THE WELL-RUN THEATRE

FORMS & SYSTEMS FOR DAILY OPERATIONS

Richard E. Schneider
Mary Jo Ford

Drama Book Publishers
New York

For their support, assistance, and contributions, the authors express their gratitude to Carol Hayes of the National Theatre, Washington, D.C., to Les Zeidel of the Elden Street Players, Herndon, Virginia, and to the many other theatre managers and box office treasurers whose expertise have helped create this book.

Printed in the United States of America.

Library of Congress Cataloging-in-Publication Data

Schneider, Richard E., 1949-
    The well-run theatre : forms & systems for daily operation /
Richard E. Schneider, Mary Jo Ford.
      p.   cm.
    ISBN 0-89676-117-7
    1. Theater management–Handbooks, manuals, etc. 2. Theater
management–Forms. I. Ford, Mary Jo, 1953- . II. Title.
PN2073.S36 1993
792'.068–dc20   91-45720
                                    CIP

Table of Contents

Introduction

No one can operate a theatre like a retail business. A regular store that does not sell its product today can sell it tomorrow. But unlike the unsold retail item, an unsold theatre ticket is a loss that can never be recovered. If you haven't been paid for tickets for a performance already given, there is nothing to repossess. Conventional business manuals, forms, and systems do not apply.

This book was developed to assist theatre operators, managers, department heads, bookkeepers, and almost everyone who works offstage in a theatre. Designed to help theatre workers do their jobs efficiently and effectively, this material is suitable for all types of theatres and performing groups, from large concert halls, opera houses, Broadway theatres, "out of town" or "road theatres," to theatres in colleges, universities, and public schools, regional theatres, local government-run theatres, and community theatres. Some theatres operate with completely unionized crews; some with paid non-union crews; and still others with volunteers who merely hope they won't spend too much of their own money. And of course, there are performing arts organizations that put on shows, but do not run the theatres they appear in. These organizations share common problems that can be solved using materials in this book. Whether large or small, box offices must account for all money taken in, including special rates, and also account for complimentary tickets. For large and small, canceled performances create many problems that must be resolved but often can be anticipated. There may be a degree of scale involved, but box office security—both from inside the organization and from outside—is a concern for all ticket selling organizations.

Each of the standard operating procedures and forms in this book has been used by theatre operators who have solved a variety of procedural problems or otherwise learned to cope with them. Each procedure offered in this book is time-tested and effective.

Of course, the forms and procedures proposed here must be adapted to the specific theatre, community, and audience. For many operations, this book presents a variety of solutions, some more complex than others. The reader should review the options offered in the book, then pick and choose what is best for his or her operation. For example, to write a contract between a theatre and a visiting attraction, review the various forms and choose one with the best applicable language, or assemble the various parts of different forms that apply in a unique and appropriate document. For payroll, office procedures, concessions, or front of house activities, this book should be used as a resource to choose what best serves the reader's needs. Many of the forms can be used right out of the book; others indicate options. If at first a form does not seem to apply to your facility because it suggests a much smaller or larger house, adding or subtracting zeros at the end of the numbers may help bring things into perspective.

One of the first questions every theatre owner must answer is what kind of operation does the owner want to run? Though there are an infinite number of variations, here are the two extremes.

First: the theatre operator who maintains a very active interest in everything that occurs in his theatre and keeps as much control as possible. For example, this theatre operator hires his own ticket sellers and lets no outside sellers handle tickets. All box office receipts are deposited into theatre controlled bank accounts, and money is transferred to the attraction's producer only when the theatre is ready to transfer it. Programs are prepared by the theatre operator, as is most of the advertising. Most stagehands, wardrobe personnel, and virtually all nonperformers who have a part in the performance are under the supervision of the theatre operator. The staff works for the theatre, regardless of who produces the show, or the type of show currently playing.

Theatre operations of this type include Broadway theatres, Broadway road houses and regional theatres.

Second: those organizations that are relatively passive, have a facility to rent, and turn it over to a producer who is then on his own. That producer must find stagehands, wardrobe, ushers, and performers. He must sell his own tickets, place his own ads, and build his own scenery. Sometimes, the theatre operator does not allow the producer to store scenery or anything else in the theatre if performances are more than a day apart.

In these theatres, if an audience member has a complaint, it is up to the producer to resolve it, not the theatre operator. There is no continuity of presentations to the public, every program is different, and every method of ticket sales is different. During the performance itself, the patron's perception often is that no one is in charge of the house.

Theatre operators of this type usually include government-owned or -operated facilities and community theatres operated by local acting groups that have no interest in any attraction other than their own.

Most organizations can be placed nearer one end of the spectrum. At some theatres, the operator will require that local stagehands be hired to maintain safety and protect the backstage equipment. Many theatres require that some tickets be sold by the theatre's own box office. This way, the theatre has control over some of the producer's money, to cover any expenses not paid for in advance.

Even the passive theatre operator should maintain a tight control over bookings and use a booking agreement that contains good self protection. Theatres that do little more than register visiting shows by a letter leave themselves open to liability, damage, and financial losses.

Regardless of management style, a performing arts organization that is poorly run in the office is often poorly run on stage and in the auditorium. This book can be used to build the professionalism and organization of the theatre. Begin with the primary location of income — the box office.

Chapter 1
The Box Office

An investigation into alleged inaccuracies in ticket counts has resulted in changes at the box office. The treasurer of the theatre resigned over the weekend, and a new treasurer was appointed.

"We discovered that the count was not entirely accurate, that the show was being shorted. We had Wells-Fargo send in 'counters' who counted the actual house and the number of tickets accounted for," said the show's producer.

The shortage was estimated at about $5,000 a week, at an average ticket price of $20.00.

— New York Times, April 11, 1979

In the struggle to produce shows and operate a facility, many small theatres and performing groups neglect the one operation that may be the key to their survival, failing to acknowledge that a poorly run box office can cause the whole theatre to fail. There are two reasons the box office is such a pivotal operation: 1) That's where the money is. 2) It is the first point of contact between the public and the theatre.

Even when public money subsidizes the theatre, ticket sales account for a high percentage of operating funds. If the box office is not properly organized, the most important source of income will be unaccountable. Without proper accounting procedures, money can be lost, misappropriated, or even stolen. If outside groups use your theatre, you may inadvertently give them your share of the box office receipts, not just theirs!

As foundation money becomes tighter and arts organizations become more sophisticated, many corporate and government grantors require adequate financial records. Some granting agencies require audited financial statements that usually require well kept box office and income records.

Even more important to a theatre's survival is the public perception of the operation. An efficient, organized, pleasant box office will encourage ticket sales. Expensive advertising and high production values may never counteract a negative experience at the box office.

The forms and procedures that follow will help organize a professional box office operation, one that avoids the embarrassment, confusion, and financial losses that can result from disorganization.

If you have a computerized box office, many forms and systems included in this chapter will still apply to you. While you do not have to prepare the basic box office statement, you will still need to document discounts, complimentary tickets, group sales, and so on.

Memorandum

To: Theatre manager and box office treasurer
Subject: Procedures prior to selling any tickets

1. Provide the manager and the treasurer with copies of all ticket orders sent to the printing company.

2. All newly printed tickets must be delivered, unopened, directly to the theatre manager.

3. Ticket boxes, still unopened, should be promptly transferred from the manager to the treasurer.

4. The original printer's manifest included with the tickets is kept by the box office treasurer, with the treasurer providing a clean carbon or photocopy to the manager.

5. The treasurer should carefully check all tickets against the manifest and the original ticket order. All tickets should be counted and checked against theatre capacity and seating charts. All printing, particularly dates, times, and prices, must be proofread. Where numerous performances make it impossible to check every individual ticket for every performance, at least check every ticket for a few different performances. In any event, always be on the lookout for anything wrong in the printing.

6. Place all tickets in ticket racks. Set aside a specific area in the rack to place tickets pulled per directions. Such location should be, for example, at the bottom of the rack for each performance, or a drawer used for no purpose other than holding tickets for current performances.

7. Pull all press, house, and company seats.

8. Pull all subscription orders.

9. Pull all group orders. Payment and pickup date must be verified and marked. There should be no overlap or conflict, but paid orders should be pulled before unpaid orders.

10. Pull all mail orders. Prepare, fill, mail, and file.

11. Pull all other standard allotments, such as telephone sales or sales through ticket agents. Availability may vary depending on advance, group, and mail order sales.

12. Box Office may now open for general sale.

13. As additional mail orders and group sales come in after the attraction goes on sale, fill the new orders in the same sequence as above. Locations may be used that have been set aside for telephone and broker sales, but only after confirmation and double checking their availability, and notice has been given to those representatives that certain locations previously assigned to them have been used.

14. All orders held at the box office, for whatever reason, must be carefully marked and readily accessible. They should also be checked before each performance, pulling out the ones for the upcoming performance, and being aware of what is there as the performance sales go on. You may, for example, write "Paid" on each paid order in a dark pen, and write the amount due with a red ink pen so they stand out. Also, note in red any refunds due for the same reason.

Form 1–1

Memorandum

To: Box office treasurer
Subject: Mail order procedures

1. When mail arrives each day, count the number of pieces of mail. This is the quickest indicator of the volume of sales. This does not reflect sales in dollars nor number of tickets, but does indicate a pattern and an average of actual sales. It also assists in tracking the effectiveness of advertising. Record the count in a permanent record and advise management of the daily count.

2. Open the mail and stamp the date received on the order.

3. With a paper clip, attach the mail order form or letter, the self-addressed, stamped envelope that should be enclosed by the patron, and the check to a box office mail order processing form (Form 1-3). Stack them letter on bottom, then envelope, then check on top.

4. Review the mail order. Make sure the cost of the tickets requested equals the amount on the check. If there is a problem with the order, fill out the mail order form *accurately!* Sometimes, if the mail order coupon is so small that you cannot write additional information on it, the order may be stapled to a form or blank piece of paper that will provide room for the necessary information to be added.

5. Some problems with orders or checks can be easily resolved by contacting the customer; use a form and process as necessary. Shows that have already closed or sold out may require returning the check to the customer. However, retain the order and make proper notation of what has occurred. When an order must be returned, or is not fillable for any reason, fill out and enclose a problem card with the order. (Form 1-4.)

6. Tickets are pulled and attached to the orders and forms. Remove and save the audit stubs from tickets that have them.

7. Ticket locations or numbers are written on the order itself or on the mail order form. Double check to make sure the orders are filled properly as to location, date, and price. The order or form is initialed by the ticket seller filling the order. Locations must also be written on the check or charge form.
    If the order contains charge account information, fill out the charge slip. The charge slip must be handled and accounted for as carefully as a check. Always get account authorization and mark the charge slip accordingly.

8. Checks and orders should be compared to make sure the names (first and last) on both match. Where they are different, write the name of the purchaser on the check. If the check bounces, you can still identify the order and contact that party.

9. A different ticket seller should separate the tickets, the return envelope, and the check (or charge slip) from the order, double checking for accuracy. The date of mailing is entered on the form, and the form is initialed again.

—(more)—

10. Each day, reconcile the audit stubs with the checks/charges. Before any tickets are mailed or checks/charges deposited, the stubs and deposit must balance.

11. Mail the tickets, deposit the checks and charges.

12. File the orders alphabetically with attached forms for future reference. Different attractions should not be filed together.

13. For quick reference, all orders should be kept separate by show and easily accessible to the ticket sellers at show time, and for several months thereafter.

14. If an order cannot be filled, return it to the sender with a card indicating the problem using (Form 1-4)

Form 1–2

Mail Order Record

Name: Check from (if different):

Address: Address:

Show_____   Special Instructions:

# of tickets_____ @ $_____

Location_____

Performance date_____

Initial_____

Date mailed_____

Initial_____

Amount Received: **Over Payment**

Check no._____   Received_____

Amount $_____   Cost of tix_____

                                         Refund due_____

Gift certificate no_____   Credit cert. no_____

Credit Card: **Under Payment**

Type_____   Received_____

Acct. no._____   Cost of tix_____

Exp. date_____   Amount due_____

Name on card_____   Buyer called on_____

                                         Buyer will_____

For reason checked below your ticket order could not be forwarded:

☐ Completely sold out (of price) (for date) specified_____
☐ Price desired available but not locations requested_____
☐ Due to limited mailing time tickets being held for mat._____eve._____
☐ Payment not correct, should be_____
☐ Please give alternate dates. _____
☐ The performance requested is not scheduled. that week_____
☐ Matinee available that day at $_____
☐ Seats available for date requested at $_____if ordered now.
☐ Failed to state date and performance_____Matinee or evening?
☐ Check returned for signature.
☐ Number of tickets and price not indicated_____
☐ Price desired not available until after_____(Sat.) (Fri.)
☐ Check with box office on arrival for possible cancellations.

Form 1–4

Memorandum

To: Box office treasurer
Subject: Box office deposits

1. Make a separate deposit slip for each attraction; whether advance sales or current attraction. On each slip write the name of the attraction, and each slip should be consecutively numbered. Keep a ledger book with a page for each show; each day enter the date of the deposit, the consecutive number of the deposit, the amount of the deposit, and a running total. Start a new series of numbers (beginning with 1) for each new show.

2. The date you write on the deposit slip should be for the day's deposit.

3. All money received that was originally listed as a receivable on a box office statement, such as ticket brokers, subscription, etc., should be clearly recorded in the ledger book and separated by attraction.

4. All deposit slips should be prepared with enough copies to provide one to all necessary personnel. The original goes to the bank with the deposit itself, while the first copy is held by the box office treasurer. Another copy may be made for the theatre manager, and where there is a separate accounting office, another copy may be needed for it. Copies may be forwarded from one office to another.

Form 1–5

Memorandum

To: Box office treasurers

Subject: Accepting checks for purchase of tickets

When a patron pays for tickets by check, please follow these procedures:

1. All checks should be preprinted with the customer's name and address.

2. The patron's day and evening telephone numbers should be written or printed on the check.

3. Preprinted information should be corroborated by examining some other identification belonging to the patron, preferably a photo I.D. such as a driver's license. Do not allow a person at the box office window to purchase tickets with someone else's check and identification. Do compare signatures on check and I.D. Of course, signatures do vary over time, so they may not match exactly. Ticket sellers have the discretion to consider other characteristics of the buyer to determine whether or not to accept the check.

4. Do not accept checks for an amount greater than the cost of the tickets. Do not give change for a check.

5. Give extra scrutiny to checks—and patrons—that have a check number lower than 100 (indicating a new account), no imprinted information, are for large sums of money, or have the account number written in by hand.

6. Always write the date of performance purchased and the exact seat locations on the check. Be sure to show specific curtain times; i.e. "7/4 mat." or "7/4 7:00."

7. Traveler's checks are acceptable if they have the first signature already in place, and the second signature is made at the window under your observation. If the second signature has already been placed, ask for a third signature. Do compare the signatures. Remember the guarantee travel companies have for replacing lost or stolen travelers checks applies only to the original buyer of the checks, not to merchants who accept them. Also, you should ask for identification even for traveler's checks.

Form 1–6

Memorandum

To: Box office treasurers

Subject: Checks returned by the bank

From time to time the bank will return checks because the check writer had insufficient funds or the account was closed. In that event, please follow these procedures:

1. Make arrangements with the bank in advance that whenever it has a returned check,

—(more)—

the bank representative should call the theatre box office with that information.

2. The treasurer should take cash from the box office drawer, go to the bank, and "buy" the check. In this manner, the original deposit slip is still correct.

3. If the performance for which the tickets were purchased has not yet been given, call the buyer and ask them to bring cash to the box office, or charge their tickets to a credit card. (Be sure to get credit card authorization!)

4. If the problem has not been corrected by the time patrons are admitted to the theatre, notify the ticket takers to watch for the specific ticket locations or numbers, so they can stop the patrons before they enter the house. The ticket takers should ask the patrons to go to the box office (before they are admitted into the theatre). If the patron gets in, before the curtain goes up have an usher go to the specific seat locations, ask for the customer by name, and tell him he has a message at the box office. The usher must not get into any discussion with the customer regarding the message.

5. Uncollected checks should be deducted from the box office statement of the attraction for which the tickets were purchased. After deduction, the original checks should be transferred to the manager for further processing.

6. Should collection eventually be made, distribution of those funds should be made according to the terms of the original agreement with the attraction for distribution of box office receipts. If the attraction has closed however, it should not appear on a box office statement.

Form 1–7

IOUS AND PETTY CASH

A box office normally operates with a certain amount of money that is used as its own "bank." It is used by the box office for buying and making change, IOUs and petty cash for theatre purposes, buying bad checks back from the bank, etc. The money comes from a manager's account, and eventually is returned to the same account. The box office cash bank needs to be large enough so that the box office can operate. Small theatres tend to think in terms of smaller amounts, but the box office must be able to conduct all its operations. Thus the bank must be scaled in accordance with the size and operational needs of the theatre. It is better to have a little more money there than less. A theatre operation looks very petty when it cannot make change for patrons. On the other hand, the organization must bear in mind the security aspects of its operations, and the potential effects were the box office robbed.

To the frustration of corporate treasurers and accountants, every theatre uses its box office as a source of petty cash. As long as this is kept under control, this is not a problem. The trick, of course, is to keep it under control.

At the end of the week or other accounting period, even after the show has closed, the box office should be able to transfer to the manager the exact amount of the gross receipts, as reported on the box office statements. To do this, all petty cash must be repaid to the box office in a timely manner.

Writing a check to reimburse petty cash establishes a permanent record so that all disbursements eventually appear on the corporate accounting books. Writing a check enables the box office to deposit money earned for receipts, enabling it to transfer money back to the manager.

While it may seem wasteful to have two branches of the same organization write checks back and forth to each other, the waste is quite minimal compared to the advantages of having a complete paper trail.

Form 1-8 is a sample box office IOU. The person requesting or receiving the money should fill it out completel/, and indicate what the money is to be used for. This is particularly useful when there are nume ous IOUs in the box office safe.

Every ope ition must decide in advance of the season or the attraction specifically who has the power to authorize IOU's and take petty cash. For the convenience—and protection—of the ticket sellers, a memo with the names of those authorized should be available. If more than one or two individuals, then the company may want to require a manager or officer to authorize the money in advance. If so, then you will want to add another signature line, one for the authorization, and another for the person who actually receives the money. IOUs and petty cash must not be authorized over the telephone.

In addition to regular theatre staff, it may be appropriate to allow company managers or producers from visiting attractions to take cash from the box office. However, this must be strictly controlled, and the manager must be kept informed of such transactions. The visitors must not be allowed to take more money than the theatre will pay under the booking contract.

Sometimes both the theatre manager and company manager are each "paying" for tickets with IOUs, subject to reimbursement. Things will be much clearer if the theatre manager takes care of his/her tickets, and the company manager takes care of his/her tickets. Neither should anticipate the other's need which leads to confusion and mistakes that cost money.

It is recommended that IOUs be printed on two-part NCR paper, or be used with carbons. Thus, when a form is used at the box office, a copy is given to the person responsible for reimbursing the box office. That is, if a staff member is authorized to take petty cash, the employee takes the cash, but the manager gets the copy for his/her records. A company manager, on the other hand, gets copies from his/her own staff.

No one is ever too busy to fill out this form. The ticket sellers who are responsible for the funds should insist on that. As they are filled out, the box office should keep them in a special folder or envelop that is used for no other purpose. There must be only one place to put the IOUs, and every IOU must be put there.

```
Date:_____

             BOX OFFICE IOU

Received from Box Office

_____   ($_____)


_____
                (Signature)

For:
```

Form 1–8

ADVANCE SALES REPORTS

Every organization will find it useful to keep track of advance sales for future performances. If you operate a computerized box office, this will be done automatically, although you may still make manual adjustments to get the information most useful for you.

If you are using a manual ticket system, you must decide how much detail of advance sales you really need, and how much work you want to put into it. The more detail you want, the more work it will take. Advance sales reports can be very complicated and time consuming.

At its most basic, the box office sells tickets by cash and carry. Deposits are made daily. After the week or performance in question, the box office transfers all its money for that period to the manager. But there is usually more than one performance being sold at a time, and sometimes tickets for more than one attraction are sold at the same time. While advance sales information for different performances of the same show may not be too important, sales reports for different attractions must be maintained, if they are to be useful to the individual producers. Detailed reports may be more important to management, press, etc., than to the box office.

There are several ways to track sales for different shows. The simplest is to keep a pad of paper by the box office window, and as a sale is made, make a note of the amount, in a different column for each show. At the end of the day, total the columns, and when making the daily bank deposit, indicate on the deposit slips the amount deposited for each attraction. Amounts recorded for each attraction represent the advance sales (which may actually include sales for current performances). Another way to separate sales for different attractions is to use two cash drawers, and just put money for whichever show into the correct drawer.

Here is an example of sales reports that would be updated as the week progresses:

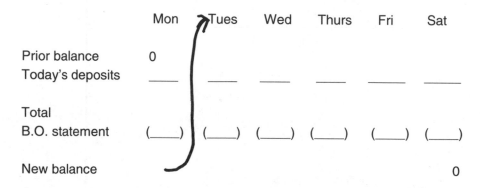

	Mon	Tues	Wed	Thurs	Fri	Sat
Prior balance	0					
Today's deposits	___	___	___	___	___	___
Total						
B.O. statement	(___)	(___)	(___)	(___)	(___)	(___)
New balance						0

Before any tickets are sold, the advance sales/prior balance must equal zero. At the end of the week, after all the performances have been given, the advance sales must also be zero.

Here is a sample of sales for shows presented on a weekend:

	Mon	Tues	Wed	Thurs	Fri	Sat
Prior balance	0	1000	2500	4500	6500	4000
Today's deposits	1000	1500	2000	2000	3500	4500
Total	1000	2500	4500	6500	10000	8500
B.O. statement	(0)	(0)	(0)	(0)	(6000)	(8500)
New balance	1000	2500	4500	6500	4000	0

Key:

The "Prior balance" is merely the amount carried forward from the previous day.

"Today's deposits" is the amount of money received by the box office each day, and actually deposited into the bank. It should reflect the actual amount on the bank deposit slips only.

The "Total" amount reflects the amount of total sales for all performances reports, minus box office sales for performances already given.

The "B.O. statement" entry reflects the official box office receipts for each performance, as reported on the individual performance statement. For purposes of this report, all performances on one day may be combined.

The "New Balance" reflects the advance sales status at the end of the day's activities. This will be the next day's "Prior Balance."

On Monday through Thursday, the box office is selling tickets for weekend performances. Every day more tickets are sold, and the advance is increasing for all the performances. However, ticket sales are reported for performances on both Friday and Saturday.

By Friday morning, the box office has taken in $6,500. During the day, an additional $3,500 of tickets are sold. That evening, the first performance is given, for a reported $6,000. Therefore, after the performance, the box office still has $4,000 available for the Saturday performances.

Saturday morning, the advance sales are $4,000. During the day an additional $4,500 is received, while the performances are valued at $8,500.

After the final performance, the advance sales is zero. No tickets have been sold to any other performances. Advance sales have equaled the actual box office statement reports.

(For additional information on the flow of money through the box office, see page 179.)

This simple system does not show which performances the advance sales are for, but its simplicity and reliability make it usable for all organizations that do not need greater detail.

Merely reporting deposits, however, may be misleading. Additional detail may have to be added. For example, accounts receivable may be a big hole in the report. If someone takes $1,000 petty cash to build scenery, and most of the sales are by credit card, there might be nothing left to deposit. Similarly, group sales contracts may have sold out a performance, but if the tickets are not yet paid for, there would be nothing to deposit. The report can be adjusted to show:

> Prior balance:
> Today's deposits:
> Accounts receivable:
> Total:

If additional detail is needed, then the list may be expanded:

> Prior balance:
> Today's deposits:
> Credit card sales:
> Groups contracted:
> IOUs:
> Total:

The marketing/press agent may not care where the money is but is interested in the source of sales. Sales trends can show the effectiveness of the advertising. Advance sales reports can help maximize advertising dollars:

Prior balance:
Window sales: _____ (from all sources)
Mail orders: _____ (from newspapers and flyers)
Telephone sales: _____ (from TV and radio)
Groups contracted: _____ (from mailing lists)
Agencies: _____ (from hotels)

Total: _____

Keeping track of individual performances or weeks at a time becomes much harder. There is a limit to how many lists you can keep next to the window. In any case, when tickets are sold through several channels, you would need lists next to the telephones, the mail orders, and so on. Similarly, numerous cash drawers would not be practical.

You may need to use audit stubs on your tickets. An audit stub is an extra stub that is torn off by the ticket seller, then properly sorted and accounted for daily. Of course, this may require additional staff to do the sorting and counting.

Additional advance sales reports from various theatre operations are shown. The possible complexity is apparent. Much of the information serves the needs of management, press, etc., more than it serves the box office.

Caveat! The ticket selling function itself requires a lot of concentration and attention to detail. It is easy for sellers to be distracted by having to remember to sort audit stubs, write down sales, or keep track of which cash drawer to use, when they really need to keep track of discounts, information on personal checks, etc. Keep priorities straight. It is better to lose information for advance sales reports than it is to lose money by errors in the ticket selling function.

Advance Sales for w/e _____

	Mon	Tues	Wed	Thurs	Fri	Sat
Prior Balance	_____	_____	_____	_____	_____	_____
Today's deposits	_____	_____	_____	_____	_____	_____
Total	_____	_____	_____	_____	_____	_____
B.O. Statement	(_____)	(_____)	(_____)	(_____)	(_____)	(_____)
New Balance	_____	_____	_____	_____	_____	_____

Form 1–9

Attraction ___

Sales on ___

	TOTAL		w/e		w/e		w/e	
	Day	Week	Day	Week	Day	Week	Day	Week
Potential								
Box Office								
Mail								
Groups Contracted								
Telephone Sales								
Brokers								
TOTAL SALES								
Less Day's Gross Receipts								
Balance of Advance								
Commissions Paid								
Net Receipts								
Sales as of one week ago								

Form 1–10

Accumulated Sales Report

Attraction:_____ Date:_____

	Today's Sales	Total to Date
Subscription	_____	_____
Mail orders	_____	_____
Box office	_____	_____
Telephones	_____	_____
Paid groups	_____	_____
Other	_____	_____
Total paid	_____	_____
Unpaid groups	_____	_____
Total Sales & Orders	_____	_____

Form 1–11

THE BOX OFFICE STATEMENT: BASIC CONCEPTS

Most community and school theatres use an additive method of determining box office sales. To determine how much money was really taken in, the box office treasurer will add up the money taken in at the window. Very often in these situations the actual number of tickets printed has never been verified. The number of tickets may be even greater than capacity. People may have taken tickets to sell outside the box office. There is usually no question of box office or individual accountability. Because few productions at this level ever sell out, these procedures generally do not present a problem.

But clearly there are potential problems with this system. Accountability of the individuals selling the tickets is difficult and hard to enforce. A meaningful, consistent system of record keeping is impossible. Reserved seats are out of the question, limiting the theatre to general admission.

Not so in the "professional" theatre. Sell outs do occur, and the accountability of the ticket sellers is under strict observance. Many people want to see reports, not the least of whom include the corporate donors—and the tax man.

Consequently, a better, more reliable system must be used. One that by its very nature resolves errors, problems, and mistakes. A system that makes people pay attention to what they are doing.

A number of factors determine which system to use. How responsible is the staff: to themselves, to the manager, to the theatre? If the money is short, who will cover the loss? If the money is short, will the manager even know it? What is the amount of the shortage? With a school or community theatre, the seating capacity, sales, and prices are not likely to be high, so the money total might not be high either. However, with lower totals, as a percentage of income, even a small loss could be devastating.

In a legitimate theatre with over a thousand seats and several weeks of sales, the dollar volume may easily reach hundreds of thousands. At this level, it is no longer possible to just add up the money and have the totals give any accurate information on the performance sales. It is impossible when checks, charges, and advance sales are involved.

Enter the subtractive method of accounting. The system, in its most basic form, works as follows. Determine the gross sales potential of a given performance, i.e. multiply the number of seats by the price of the ticket, including all the price ranges and different seating areas. Assume full price on all sales. The result equals the total potential sales (Form 1-12). For each performance, you add up the money taken in at the box office, just as in the amateur style discussed above. If the show has sold out at full price, the two numbers—potential money and real money—should be equal. Any difference must be an error, whether the money is short or over.

In the subtractive system, the manager's basic approach is to say to the box office treasurer, "Prove to me you did not sell out at full price." That is all there is to it. As long as this question is addressed, any other questions about the performance should fall into place.

To provide the proof, the treasurer must produce materials and back up the premise that there was no sellout. The first and simplest proof is deadwood, the unsold tickets. The treasurer is now saying, "I can prove I did not sell out, here are the unsold tickets to prove it." Complimentary tickets may be accounted for by the ticket order form authorizing no charge. Because the actual tickets are taken by the customer, they are not available to be part of the proof, but the complimentary seat orders are available. The order form is the proof that those tickets identified on the form were not sold at full price.

Now it becomes more complicated as more ticket sale prices and arrangements are added. Special rates—usually discount tickets sold to students, senior citizens, subscribers or groups—are paid for, but not at full price. On the statement they must be identified as tickets "not sold at full price." Because the tickets are gone, they are not deadwood. Thus, elsewhere on the statement, usually below the main/full price section, they must be added back in at the price there were actually sold for (Form 1-13).

There are only three not sold at full price categories: deadwood, complimentary, and special rates. Most box office statements are designed with a place where these categories may be totaled. This total is subtracted from the capacity and shows the number of tickets sold at full price.

The Well-Run Theatre

Non-computer box office statements should be "proved" after preparation. This is a double check against hitting a wrong number on a calculator or writing a number down incorrectly.

Start with "Net this Performance," add back in credit card and other commissions, and add in how much you have lost on all the discount and complimentary tickets. The total should be the potential gross for that performance if every ticket was sold for full price.

It is important to note that the seating capacity listed on the statement must equal the permanent number of seats available, which must equal the number of tickets printed. This policy is not restricted to hard (i.e. reserved seat) tickets. When a show requires removing some seats from the auditorium, the capacity shown on the official ticket manifest from the ticket company does not change. If there is no manifest, refer to the normal, theoretical gross potential sales. In any case, the seats are "killed"—made unavailable for sale to anyone.

In school theatres, where nonreserved tickets are often printed in the school or by commercial printers rather than ticket companies, there is no official manifest. Commercial printers guarantee the number of items requested, with as much as ten percent overrun. Therefore, it is usually a number greater than capacity. In this situation, use the auditorium seating capacity as the standard number. It is important to have a consistent base number to use for comparison and accounting purposes.

Note: when you receive the tickets from a local printer, count them. Set aside the exact number of tickets you need, then destroy any overage. Do not just throw them in the trash.

If you must use an additive system, you can still use the basic box office statement form. Try to use many of the features found in the other system. You will determine the number of tickets sold at different prices, so work backward to fill out the form. Enter the number sold at full price, then discounts and passes. Subtract that from the seating capacity to get the theoretical amount of deadwood.

The calculator used in the box office should have a printed paper tape. This is a big help in double checking the computations and helps identify when a wrong key is punched, or a decimal point or extra zero is entered in the wrong place. A tape listing all checks may also be attached to a deposit, eliminating the need to manually enter each check.

At the box office window, keep a price scale chart. List ticket prices across the top, and numbers one through ten down the left side. Multiply the figures out, and with a glance the ticket seller can tell, for example, the cost of seven tickets at $8.50. It is faster than constantly multiplying each customer's order, and helps avoid mistakes.

Remember to repeat the date/time/name of attraction to the customer as you hand over the tickets. At the box office window, post a sign that says:

PLEASE EXAMINE TICKETS CAREFULLY

NO REFUNDS - NO EXCHANGES

Price Scale

Name of Attraction

Tuesday through Thursday and Sunday Evenings at 7:30 p.m.

Orchestra	A-G	150	6.00	900.00
Orchestra	H-T	100	5.00	500.00
Balcony		<u>150</u>	4.00	<u>600.00</u>
		400		2,000.00

Four performances @ $2,000.00.... $8,000.00

Friday and Saturday Evenings at 7:30 p.m.

Orchestra	A-G	150	7.00	1,050.00
Orchestra	H-T	100	6.00	600.00
Balcony		<u>150</u>	5.00	<u>750.00</u>
		400		2,400.00

Two performances @ $2,400.00.... 4,800.00

Saturday and Sunday Matinees at 2:00 p.m.

Orchestra	A-G	150	5.00	750.00
Orchestra	H-T	100	4.00	400.00
Balcony		<u>150</u>	3.00	<u>450.00</u>
		400		1,600.00

Two performances @ $1,600.00.... 3,200.00

Gross Potential for Eight Performances: $16,000.00

Form 1–12

BOX OFFICE STATEMENT

Day_____   Date _____

Weather_____   ☐ Mat.   ☐ Eve. at _____

Attraction_____   Performance No._____   Week No. _____

LOCATION	CAPACITY	DEAD WOOD	COMPS	SPECIAL RATES	TOTAL UNSOLD	SOLD	PRICE		AMOUNT	
TOTALS										

HARDWOOD			OPENING NUMBER	CLOSING NUMBER				

SPECIAL RATES	REG. PRICE	%			SOLD	PRICE	AMOUNT		
TOTALS									

We hereby certify that the undersigned have personally
checked the above statement and it is in every way correct.

SUBTOTAL

_____

BOX OFFICE TREASURER

NET THIS PERF.

_____

THEATRE MANAGER

PREV. TOTAL

TOTAL TO DATE

_____

COMPANY MANAGER

Form 1-13

BOX OFFICE STATEMENT

Day_____ Date _____

Weather_____ ☐ Mat. ☐ Eve. at _____

Attraction_____ Performance No._____ Week No. _____

LOCATION	CAPACITY	DEAD WOOD	COMPS	SPECIAL RATES	TOTAL UNSOLD	SOLD	PRICE		AMOUNT	
Orch A - G	150	8	2	74	84	66	6	00	396	00
H - T	100	46	0	32	78	22	5	00	110	00
Balcony	150	27	0	76	103	47	4	00	188	00
TOTALS	400	81	2	182	265	135			694	00

HARDWOOD		OPENING NUMBER	CLOSING NUMBER				

SPECIAL RATES	REG. PRICE	%			SOLD	PRICE		AMOUNT	
Subscription	6.00	25%			0	4	50	0	00
SPT: A - G	6.00	50%			24	3	00	72	00
H - T	5.00	50%			32	2	50	80	00
Balcony	4.00	50%			76	2	00	152	00
Groups	6.00	20%			50	4	80	240	00
TOTALS					182			544	00	544	00

We hereby certify that the undersigned have personally
checked the above statement and it is in every way correct.

SUBTOTAL	1238	00
5% Groups	⟨12	00⟩
5% Credit Card	⟨20	00⟩
NET THIS PERF.	1206	00
PREV. TOTAL		
TOTAL TO DATE		

BOX OFFICE TREASURER

THEATRE MANAGER

COMPANY MANAGER

Form 1-14

The Well-Run Theatre

BOX OFFICE STATEMENT

Day_____ Date_____

Weather_____ ☐ Mat. ☐ Eve. at_____

Attraction_____ Performance No._____ Week No._____

LOCATION	CAPACITY	DEAD WOOD	COMPS	SPECIAL RATES	TOTAL UNSOLD	SOLD	PRICE			AMOUNT
TOTALS										

We hereby certify that the undersigned have personally checked the above statement and it is in every way correct.

SUBTOTAL			

_____

BOX OFFICE TREASURER

_____

THEATRE MANAGER

NET THIS PERF.			
PREV. TOTAL			
TOTAL TO DATE			

_____

COMPANY MANAGER

Form 1-15

BOX OFFICE STATEMENT

Day_____ Date_____
Weather_____ ☐ Mat. ☐ Eve. at_____
Attraction_____ Performance No._____ Week No._____

LOCATION	CAPACITY	DEAD WOOD	COMPS	SPECIAL RATES	TOTAL UNSOLD	SOLD	PRICE		AMOUNT	
Orch A-G	150	8	2							
Full Price						66	6	00	396	00
Subscription				25%		0	4	50	0	00
SPT				50%		24	3	00	72	00
Groups				20%		50	4	80	240	00
Orch H-T	100	46	0							
Full Price						22	5	00	110	00
SPT				50%		32	2	50	80	00
Balcony	150	27								
Full Price						47	4	00	188	00
SPT				50%		76	2	00	152	00
TOTALS	400	81	2			317				

We hereby certify that the undersigned have personally
checked the above statement and it is in every way correct.

SUBTOTAL	1238	00
5% Groups	⟨12	00⟩
5% Credit Card	⟨20	00⟩

_____
BOX OFFICE TREASURER

_____
THEATRE MANAGER

_____
COMPANY MANAGER

NET THIS PERF.	1206	00
PREV. TOTAL		
TOTAL TO DATE		

Form 1-16

The Well-Run Theatre

ALTERNATE FORM OF BOX OFFICE STATEMENT

If most of your sales are full-price tickets, then the box office statement in Form 1-13 is probably best for you. If most of your sales are discounts, then Form 1-15 has some advantages. As you can see from the filled out version, Form 1-13 shows at a glance total full price sales, and total discount sales. Form 1-15 shows at a glance how many tickets in each seating area or price section were sold. If you compare each set of numbers, you can see that each form contains the same information, only set forth in a different manner.

ROLL TICKETS: A SYSTEM FOR SMALLER THEATRES

In a computerized box office, the cost to print the tickets themselves may not be an issue. But buying professional quality theatre tickets from one of the commercial ticket companies can be a significant cost. If you use commercially printed tickets, with or without reserved seats, the printing cost may run into hundreds of dollars each month. If virtually all sales are at the time of performance, with no advance sales, and the performances do not sell out, or rarely come close to selling many tickets, this seems to be a tremendous waste of money.

There is another way.

Some companies produce tickets in rolls of 1,000 or 2,000 per roll. The least expensive are carnival type tickets that might cost as little as $5.00 for one thousand tickets. There are also theatre type tickets available on a roll. Of course the tickets are not dated and will not have the attraction name, but you can special order rolls with the theatre name printed on the tickets. If you are ordering tickets, have a price printed on them. All tickets on a roll will have the same price printed on them, but the cost is low enough that you can order several different rolls for different prices. Be sure to use different color tickets for each price. Each ticket on a roll has its own serial number, which enables the treasurer to keep track of individual tickets. Obviously, reserved seats are impossible. For special priced tickets, you can use different rolls at the same time that are different colors. This makes keeping track of discounts quite easy.

If you have a small operation that virtually never sells out, then using undated roll tickets may work for you. It will work best if all sales are walk up sales at the time of the performance. The box office would open at 6:00 p.m. or so for evening performances (some places merely open one half hour before the scheduled curtain time), and noon for matinees. In this situation, you would do a box office statement the way old movie houses used to do it, without a capacity, and using opening and closing numbers. With undated tickets you cannot really tell people they can only come to one specific performance. However, you can exercise some control over the abuse of using weekday price tickets on a weekend, by color coding that change in price. A good idea would be to identify on the price scale posted at the window the color, e.g. "Friday—Saturday $8.00 (Blue)" and "Sunday—Thursday $6.00 (Red)". A problem is that handling several rolls of tickets in a box office can be cumbersome and lead to mistakes. Multiple rolls would also be necessary if there is more than one full price in the theatre, or separate seating levels.

Reminder: if you sell many tickets for future performances, this system may cause problems in tracking sales and attendance. Using roll tickets is practical only if most sales are made at the time of the performance.

Avoid selling tickets without prices printed on them. Whether the customer pays $5.00 or $50.00

for one ticket, that ticket is a receipt, and when the ticket seller accepts a certain amount of money in payment for tickets, the customer should receive back tickets that are individually correctly priced (or marked to indicate the discount) and that the customer can check before walking away from the box office window.

Procedures:

1. Before the box office starts selling tickets each day, record the serial number of the first ticket on the end of the roll. Enter that number on the box office statement (Form 1-16) at "opening number" under the section marked "Hardwood." Sell tickets by taking each ticket off the end of the roll.

2. At the conclusion of all sales for that performance, record the number of the next ticket left on the roll, that is, the ticket that will be sold first for the next performance. Record this number on the statement under "closing number."

3. Subtract the opening from the closing number to determine the number sold. Multiply the number sold times the price and enter the amount on the statement. If every ticket was sold at full price, this amount is your gross receipts.

4. A subtractive accounting system still works with roll tickets, and the "prove you did not sell out at full price" requirement also works. But instead of adding in the amount of the discounts, with roll tickets you subtract the amount discounted. Form 1-17 can be used with this system.

5. On the box office statement, make no entries in the top portion of the paper.

6. Prepare each discounted ticket just as you would a regular, non-roll ticket. In the section marked "Special Rates," indicate the type of discount (SPT, group, complimentary, etc.); the regular full price, the percent of the full price discounted, the number sold, and the actual amount of discount per ticket. The number sold times the actual discount equals the value of the total deduction. Subtract that amount from the total amount derived in #3, above. The result is the actual gross receipts for that performance.

7. Account for complimentary tickets in the same way. The value of the discount is 100 percent, so the full price and the deduction value is the same.

8. As with other systems, subtract from the gross sales any commissions for credit cards, group sales, taxes, and so on. The balance is the "Net This Performance."

9. Backup documentation is the same as in other systems.

10. The closing number from one performance as written on the last box office statement must be the opening number for the next performance. Make no exceptions. If you observe that tickets are missing, they must be accounted for as a shortage. Where are they? Who took them? Who will be using them? Will they be used for admission at a performance? Or will someone try to return them for an exchange or refund? Who has access to your tickets and might take tickets without proper authorization or documentation?

The Well-Run Theatre

BOX OFFICE STATEMENT

Day_____ Date _____
Weather_____ ☐ Mat. ☐ Eve. at _____
Attraction_____ Performance No._____ Week No. _____

LOCATION	CAPACITY	DEAD WOOD	COMPS	SPECIAL RATES	TOTAL UNSOLD	SOLD	PRICE		AMOUNT	
TOTALS										

HARDWOOD		OPENING NUMBER	CLOSING NUMBER							
Orch A - G		001	143	142	6	00		852	00	
H - T		101	155	54	5	00		270	00	
Balcony		201	324	123	4	00		492	00	
				319				1614	00	

SPECIAL RATES	REG. PRICE	%			SOLD	PRICE		AMOUNT		
Orch A - G	6.00	0%	N/C		2	6	00	⟨12 00⟩		
	6.00	50%	SPT		24	3	00	⟨72 00⟩		
	6.00	25%	Sub.		0	1	50	0 00		
	6.00	20%	Group		50	1	20	⟨60 00⟩		
Orch H - T	5.00	50%	SPT		32	2	50	⟨80 00⟩		
Balcony	4.00	50%	SPT		76	2	00	⟨152 00⟩		
TOTALS					106			⟨376 00⟩	⟨376 00⟩	

We hereby certify that the undersigned have personally checked the above statement and it is in every way correct.

SUBTOTAL		1238 00
5% Group		⟨12 00⟩
5% Credit Card		⟨20 00⟩
NET THIS PERF.		1206 00
PREV. TOTAL		
TOTAL TO DATE		

_____
BOX OFFICE TREASURER

_____
THEATRE MANAGER

COMPANY MANAGER

Form 1-17

BOX OFFICE STATEMENT

Date_____ Time_____

Attraction_____

Type	No. of Tickets	Price	Total
Regular	_____	_____	_____
Students	_____	_____	_____
Senior Citizens	_____	_____	_____
Complimentary	_____	_____	_____
Groups	_____	_____	_____
Season Tickets	_____	_____	_____
_____	_____	_____	_____
_____	_____	_____	_____
Totals	_____		_____

Box Office Treasurer_____

THE LITTLE BOX OFFICE

As indicated earlier, a simple, additive method of determining box office sales is inappropriate for all but the smallest operations. Consequently, for those smaller events, or for those organizations that for various reasons find it difficult to prepare a regular, audit-proof statement, we revisit that old additive system.

There is not much to explain. On Form 1-18, the number of tickets sold at each price is reported to the box office treasurer. Usually, there is little back-up documentation for discounts, except for lists kept by individual ticket sellers or prices circled on the sold tickets. Capacity is not reported, whether or not the number of tickets printed equals the number of seats in the house.

For each type of ticket sold, enter the number sold, multiply by its price, and total the value. That equals the gross receipts.

It is possible to provide some security. If students or friends or cast members walk around trying to sell tickets, record the number of tickets given to each person. If Johnny is given ten tickets to sell at $5.00, then he should return either $50.00 or ten tickets, or a combination of the two. If he is allowed to sell discounts, then you may have to take his word for what he actually sold. It would be better to have discounts broken down for time of sale, such as tickets sold in advance for one price, and tickets sold at the door at another price. This avoids the problem of individuals handling their own discounts.

HOUSE SEATS

"House seats" refer to a specific location, not price. Any seat in the house can be given away, but usually only specific seats are house seats. Confusion, costing the house money when tickets that should have been paid for are given away, can be avoided if all concerned keep this distinction in mind.

Before tickets go on sale to anyone, some tickets for use by management should be pulled from the rest of the tickets and set aside in the box office. Where there are reserved seats, these house seats are usually the same seat locations for all performances. Usually there are three groups of locations held for specific purposes. One group, normally called "house" seats, are held for use by the theatre manager. These are used for special patrons (benefactors, politicians, etc.) of the theatre, and to solve some seating problems that arise with the general public. The theatre's press agent has "press" seats held for use by critics and others who provide special services for press and public relations. The visiting attraction usually has tickets set aside under the control of the company manager. These "company" seats are available for the benefit of the stars of the show and for those who provide special services for the attraction. For each of these categories, one person should be responsible for the assignment of seats. There is no overlap, and one manager cannot use seats assigned to another. For the convenience of this book, all such collections of seats will be referred to as "house" seats.

Which seats should be held? The answer is highly variable. There are no fixed requirements but there are recommendations. For example, on opening night, the press seats should include numerous pairs of seats on aisles. Traditionally, media critics preferred aisle seats so that they could rush out of the theatre at the end of the show to write their reviews for the morning papers. The urgency seems to be reduced these days, but the preference remains. The theatre manager's seats should include perhaps four seats in each of two rows, one right behind the other, on an aisle. Thus a block of eight seats is created. Additionally, there probably should be one or two non-adjacent pairs on the other side of the house, also on an aisle. Finally, if the theatre is presenting a new show, or one which has a director or producer in regular attendance, one pair of center aisle seats in the very last row is helpful. The company seats may have to be set in conformance with the contractual agreements with the stars of the show. These also are likely to be center aisle seats, and may total one or even two dozen seats.

Be sure to designate several pairs of accessible aisle seats, different aisles, for disabled patrons.

How many seats should be set aside? That will vary with many elements. The obvious question to be answered is, "how many seats has the theatre traditionally needed?" For most shows, are the house seats all used up most at performances, or are dozens of seats released every day right before the performance? In a Broadway-sized playhouse, there may be easily a total of twenty to forty seats saved for every performance.

While as a matter of convenience the same seats should be assigned for every performance for every attraction (except for opening night, when many more press seats will be needed), different attractions will have different demands. Before a show goes on sale, an expected hit show will need to hold more seats, while a tired rerun will need fewer.

It is important that the various staffs be alert to the degree of use of their seats. It is pretty bad to have twenty or thirty unused house seats released for sale at the box office one half hour before curtain time. The distribution of patrons in the house will look rather peculiar if none of the best seats in the house are sold. Consequently, availability of house seats should be reviewed constantly. For some shows, it may become apparent early in the run that not all seats are ever going to be used for any one performance. Therefore, some of the held seats should be released as far in advance as is comfortable, so that the box office can sell them, and thereby avoid having the best seats in the house vacant for a performance. Additionally, the night before each performance, most remaining seats should be released for sale, retaining only that number of seats that might reasonably be needed on the last day at performance time for last minute requests that must be filled.

Each theatre should establish firmly the rule that only one person has control of the assignment of seats in any category, and that other staff members should not be able to ask the box office for any of those seats, for any purpose.

Each person responsible for house seats, including press agents and managers, should keep a running record of house seats they distribute. In this manner, they can keep track of their seats at all times. This also avoids assigning the same seats to two different sets of people—which can be a real problem when the show is sold out.

Smaller theatres that use non-reserved seats still should keep a list, albeit without seat numbers, in order to keep track of what they are doing, and for whom. Even without reserved seats, duplicate orders are to be avoided.

Keep house seat orders on hand in the box office during the run of the show because there is always the possibility of confusion over dates. When a show is selling out, there will be a similar run on house seats. Consequently, it is entirely possible that the requestor's first choice of dates is not available. Thus, confusion may exist. When a patron arrives for his front and center seats on November 10th, but his order was actually for November 5th, there will be unhappy people. Having the past date order does not help find seats for a later date, but at least the box office will know why there is no order for that night's performance.

Form 1-19: Each individual ticket that is assigned for use as a house seat must be recorded. When using reserved seats, as in this sample form, the assigned seats are usually permanently assigned, so it is easy to prepare the form in bulk. The form is simple to use. Just prepare one copy for each performance, and place it in a notebook. When setting up the book for each new production, one need only circle the day and time, and enter the date of the future performance. Even if non-reserved seat tickets are used, hold and record the serial number of several tickets. While actual seat locations are not reserved, the number of tickets to be used is still recorded. Adjustments are easily made for single or other odd orders.

When filling house seats orders, there are three payment options. In the first, the person using the tickets must pick them up and pay no later than twenty-four hours (or some other specified time) before the performance, at which time the tickets should be automatically released.

Suggestion: as the deadline approaches, contact the person who requested the tickets and ask if he wants to guarantee them. This saves arguments.

For the second, the person ordering the tickets can guarantee that they will be paid for, even if they are never used. However, this method should be avoided. If the performance has passed, and the tickets have not been paid for, how can you really get the money from the guarantor? If you cannot enforce the guarantee without cooperation from the guarantor, do not accept the order. It should be clear, collection is the obligation of the guarantor, not the theatre. The guarantor is not permitted to report, "Well, the guy just won't pay for them." If the guy won't pay, the guarantor must pay. A safer approach is to have the guarantor provide a credit card number in advance. If the guy does not show, charge the guarantor's account.

Third, the tickets may be complimentary. "No charge" or "n/c" must be written in. (Complimentary tickets will be discussed in the next section.)

Fourth, have the guest phone in his or her own credit card number.

Of course, individual theatre operators must adapt these techniques to suit their own situation.

House seat orders that have not been paid for can become a problem as well, especially when the show is selling out. (Many of these potential problems are only academic when the show does not sell out. So long as there are other tickets to sell, it is less important which tickets are sold.) After the pickup/payment deadline has passed, contact the person requesting the tickets, usually the manager or press agent. That person may decide to extend the deadline; if so, make a note right on the order. If the seller is told to cancel the order, write on the order "Cancelled by _____" and note the date and time it was canceled. When tickets are canceled, the tickets are placed back in the rack, to either be sold or included in deadwood.

The ticket sellers must always go through their reservations before each performance and be absolutely certain that all reservations for that performance have been located, both paid and not paid. Unpaid orders left over after a sell out are not just worthless, they have actually cost the theatre money when they could have been sold. They are lost income that can never be made up. Tickets are not mere pieces of paper, they are money. An unpaid and unpicked up order with the tickets still attached shows up on the box office statement as sold tickets! But no money has been collected to pay for them, so the box office will be short.

Forms 1-20 and 1-21 are forms used to assign house seats. Form 1-20 is more traditional. This form is filled out by an authorized person, then given to the recipient to be taken to the box office to pick up the tickets. Form 1-21 is similar, but the order form is taken by theatre staff directly to the box office. The recipient of the tickets still must go to the box office and request the tickets. With Form 1-20, the convenience is that the customer carries the paper work. With Form 1-21, the paper work is completed at the convenience of the box office, rather than when the tickets are picked up, avoiding potential problems at a busy time.

Both forms are excellent in their clarity and simplicity, provided all appropriate information is properly entered. "Ordered by" is the person requesting the tickets, such as the star of the show or the press agent. "For" is the name of the ultimate user, and the box office should file the order in that name. The "ordered by" name should be recognizable by the box office staff and the manager, the "for" name can be anyone.

Proper use of the forms helps avoid potential problems. Sometimes when a person asks for tickets in a certain name, the box office cannot find the order. The ticket seller should then ask how the tickets were ordered. Upon learning that they were ordered by the press agent, for example, the seller can call the press office and hear that the tickets were left in the name of the first string critic, not the second stringer that the newspaper assigned. The order is found; problem solved. In a different situation, the ticket seller sees that the tickets "ordered by" the star of the show have not yet been picked up as performance time approaches. A call backstage brings the announcement that the star meant to cancel the order, but forgot to tell anyone. The tickets are released, problem solved.

Note that the forms are still designed for paid tickets, not complimentary. The number of tickets to be used times proper price equals total due. If the tickets are to be free, mark the number of tickets, and enter "n/c" as total due.

The individual responsible for assigning the house seats, or having the authority to issue free tickets, must authorize the order. This is a manager, or company manager, or press agent, but rarely anyone else.

The Well-Run Theatre

HOUSE SEATS		

M   T   W   T   F   Sat   Sun   mat.

eve.   Date_____

Locations	For	Ordered By	How Paid
D 101-102			
D 103-104			
E 101-102			
E 103-104			
F 2-4			
F 1-3			

Form 1-19

SEAT ORDER

Attraction

Ordered By

For

No. & Location

Day & Date — Mat / Eve

No. _____ x $ _____ = Total Due

If not called for, release by:

☐ 24 Hours ☐ 6PM (noon) ☐ Guaranteed

Authorized By

Kindly sign below to acknowledge receipt of tickets.

Form 1-21

HOUSE SEAT ORDER

(Attraction)

IMPORTANT: Tickets Must Be Picked Up No Later Than 6:00 PM on Business Day Before the Date Specified Below. If Not, This Order is Automatically Cancelled.

For

No. & Location

Date — Mat / Eve

Amount Due

Tickets Authorized By _____

Present this order at the Box Office
NO TICKETS WILL BE RELEASED WITHOUT THIS ORDER!

Kindly sign below to acknowledge receipt of tickets when surrendering this order at the box office.

Tickets Received By _____

Form 1-20

The Well-Run Theatre

COMPLIMENTARY TICKETS

All tickets must always be accounted for. If the ticket is not in the box office at the time a performance statement is finalized, the ticket is considered sold at full price—unless the ticket seller can prove that the ticket was not sold. Consequently, there must be a paper trail for all complimentary tickets, regardless of the reason the ticket was given away. Whether for press, public relations, or friends of the stars of the show, the paperwork is the same.

This applies to all box office systems, whether hard tickets or computer operations. For a computer system, the machine may account for the lack of money in the cash drawer, but the ticket seller must still justify the free ticket.

Form 1-22 is a standardized procedure for creating the paper trail for complimentary tickets. Note that with computer generated tickets it may not be necessary to punch holes in the free tickets, as the price printed on the ticket should indicate "$0.00," or the word "Complimentary."

The individual, original complimentary seat orders (Forms 1-20 or 1-21), when used for free tickets, must be attached to the performance box office statement. They are part of the proof by the treasurer that the show was not sold out at full price. House seats that are sold at full price become irrelevant to the statement, so those orders are not included with the sales reports. Nevertheless, it is wise to save even those orders until the end of the engagement, in case questions arise concerning authorized use of seats, mistakes at a later date, and so on.

Information concerning "no shows" should be kept at the box office window, so that if the party appears at a later date, the problem can be identified promptly. For convenience, just keep the empty ticket envelope available.

When there are many seat orders, such as for an opening night, a summary order list, Form 1-23, is made up and attached to the statement. This list carries no individual weight for the proof, but is merely a convenience to the treasurer and manager in keeping track of all the orders.

Just as it is important that only one person be authorized to assign house seats, it is even more important that only one person (for each category) be authorized to give free tickets. This rule must be strictly enforced by both management and the box office. The ticket sellers do not want to be in the position of guessing that some person at the window is important enough to get a free ticket, because if they guess wrong, they may be held responsible for the lost income. Consequently, the manager must not send a person to the box office for free seats, when an order form has not been properly prepared. As part of the preparation of the form, regardless of who actually fills out the information for names, dates, etc., only the manager (or press agent) may sign it. No one else. Because the box office actually has possession of the tickets, it can enforce the policy, but the manager had better back them up.

Do note that many booking contracts contain language such as "the free admission, except to local press, shall be by mutual agreement." This means that the press agent can have critics invited, but neither the theatre manager nor the company manager can give tickets to anyone else, unless the other agrees. Usually the two managers have an "understanding," but the contract language, if ignored, can produce expensive mistakes of expectations.

Memorandum

To: Box office treasurer
Subject: Complimentary tickets

1. The manager or press agent should fill out a (house) seat order form, including either the specific seat or ticket numbers, then record this information in the House Seat record book. (Form 1-19.) This form is then sent to the box office.

2. The box office receives the form, pulls the tickets, and writes the date of the tickets, the price (face value) of the tickets, and the specific seat locations on the form, and the amount due or "n/c." This duplicates what the manager has written, but it forces the ticket seller to actually look at the tickets in hand, thereby providing a double check on what is going out. The actual tickets are pulled from the rack and, with a hand held paper hole puncher, each ticket is punched at both ends, and on the audit stub, if used. If the box office computer prints the tickets with an indication of no charge, then punching or other marks is not necessary.

3. The tickets are left at the window with the order, which must be signed by the patron ("Received by_____") when the tickets are picked up. The patron gets the tickets, the box office keeps the order form.

4. A summary page of all complimentary orders is made up by the box office, providing a single page list of all such tickets for that performance. A summary list is not necessary if there are few individual orders.

5. Both the individual seat orders and the summary list (if created) of orders is provided as backup documentation for the box office statement.

6. The tickets are torn at the door by the ticket taker, and the drop count verifies the number of punched tickets shown on the statement.

7. Complimentary tickets not picked up may either be a) left at the window as "no shows" for the run of the engagement, or b) stapled to the bottom of the house seat order over the line for the signature of the patron. In either case, the order itself must accompany the box office statement.

8. If patrons holding complimentary tickets try to exchange the tickets, tell them to speak with the individual who provided the tickets in the first place.

9. If complimentary tickets are punched and ready to be picked up and then canceled for any reason, the complimentary markings on the tickets must be canceled, and the tickets returned to the ticket rack. On the back of the ticket, draw a circle around the hole, and the person marking the ticket should place his or her initials beside the circle. The ticket should be placed in the ticket rack for sale. Be sure to change the seat order to reflect the comp order that was canceled. Note who canceled it, and when.

Form 1–22

The Well-Run Theatre

	Ticket Order Summary		
Date			
Attraction			

No.	Name	Arranged By	Location

Form 1-23

In non-professional theatre, many performers believe they are entitled to free tickets. This may be the policy of the organization, but there should be unambiguous instructions written to all personnel, and to the box office, setting forth exactly what the policy is, and what the procedures are.

Sometimes people try to return comps for a refund (or try to sell them to other people). You must be careful never to refund a ticket that was not paid for.

SPECIAL PRICED TICKET PROGRAMS

Many theatre organizations, especially non-profits, make it possible for certain groups of people to purchase tickets at less than the regular full price, through some sort of Special Price—or Patron—Ticket program ("SPT"). These groups usually include students, but may also include senior citizens, military, lower income people, or disabled people. Which categories of people are to be included is completely at the discretion of the organization. But regardless of who can buy discount tickets, how the paperwork is handled presents problems for all theatres, and varies little with hard ticket or computer operations.

How does the ticket seller determine which individuals are allowed to buy a discount ticket? If the decision is not made by the ticket seller, who makes it? What specific criteria may be used to determine eligibility? For example, if students can buy SPTs, what grade or age is the cut off—high school? College? Graduate school? Anyone with a current student registration card? What about adults who are taking a few courses in a night program? All these details must be decided in advance.

Is there a limit to the number of SPTs that may be sold for any performance or engagement? How can ticket sellers keep track of the number sold when selling several performances at once? What kind of accounting will the treasurer have that these tickets were not sold at full price? How can management determine that when proof of discount is provided, the tickets were really sold for that price, and that the ticket seller is accurately accounting for the money?

How are the tickets marked when sold to the customer? Can something be done to hinder a person from buying SPTs and reselling them for full price? If the box office has to make a refund, will it be clear that the refund will only be for the discounted price, and not for the full price?

With a computer operation the tickets are likely to be printed with the actual SPT price, and possibly marked "student" or otherwise. But almost all of the other problems remain.

Form 1-24 shows one theatre's plan for an SPT program. This system is extensive, offering discount tickets to six categories of patrons. Note the detail that has been developed for the staff and public. The classifications are quite specific and well defined. There is little room for dispute about anyone's eligibility.

When staffing permits, many larger theatres have found it best to have someone outside the box office make the eligibility determination. Form 1-25 has instructions for the person qualifying patrons. Note that for this system of control, Forms 1-26 or 1-27 are used for the treasurer's proof of discount.

The Well-Run Theatre

Sometimes a theatre group does not have the luxury of having a box office available before performance time or must have many people sell tickets, some of whom will not be well trained in the art of ticket sales. Or perhaps the operator merely wants a very easy-to-use system. In these circumstances, some groups have their tickets printed with both the full price and the discount price on the ticket, the stub, and the third part audit stub. When a ticket is sold, the seller circles the selling price on the three parts. The seller then tears off and keeps the audit stub. This stub is used by the seller to account for what he sold, and it is carefully turned over to the head ticket seller. The audit stub provides the only information available to the box office that a ticket was sold for a certain price.

But watch out! An unscrupulous seller could circle the lesser price, sell it for full price, and pocket the difference. The office might never find out.

EASY AND ACCOUNTABLE

The box office can tighten up on some of these loopholes. For example, see Form 1-26. This is good for a small theatre that does not have a concern with box office security, only accounting. Consequently, they use the following steps:

1. A patron presents proof of eligibility to the ticket seller.

2. The seller and patron select a performance.

3. The seller rubber stamps the date of the performance on the coupon, and checks the box of the category of SPT patron, thus providing a means to track the nature of the audience.

4. The seller tears from the ticket only the audit stub, and staples that stub to the coupon. This becomes the seller's proof of discount sold. (Under these circumstances, audit stubs cannot be used also to determine advance sales.)

5. The seller punches holes in the ticket (different shaped holes from those used to identify complimentary tickets) to identify it as a discount. The customer walks away with a whole ticket (not including the audit stub), but no coupon attached.

6. At performance time, the ticket taker tears off the stub as if it were any other ticket.

COMPLICATED BUT SECURE

This last system utilized with Form 1-27 is cumbersome and time consuming. Used to its full application, the process works like this for a non-computerized box office.

1. The patron goes to the people who are making eligibility determinations.

2. The patron proves his or her qualifications.

3. The staff person prepares one or two coupons, entering the patron's name and the name of the attraction. The ticket price and the performance date is left blank at this time.

4. The patron takes the coupons to the box office and requests tickets.

5. If the ticket seller and the patron agree on a performance date and seating area, then the ticket seller prepares one or two SPT tickets. If they cannot agree on a performance—remember SPT's may be limited in number for any one performance—then the patron either pays full price or does not buy tickets. Either way, the coupon is no longer necessary, and should be destroyed by the box office.

6. If a performance is agreed to, the seller takes a ticket, and rubber stamps "SPT" on the back of the ticket so that it is visible from every portion of the ticket. (But if there is more than one discount rate, the exact price of the ticket must be stamped on the ticket. There must never be any doubt what price was paid.)

7. The seller takes one coupon and one ticket, and tears or cuts each in two pieces. To the stub end of the ticket, the small portion of the coupon is stapled, the large portion of the ticket is stapled to the large part of the SPT form.

8. The customer leaves with the large portion, the seller keeps the small portions as proof of a ticket sold at discount. This remains with the box office statement.

9. At performance time, the customer presents what he holds: half a ticket stapled to half a coupon. The ticket taker separates the two parts, keeping the coupon portion, and returning the ticket portion to the patron.

10. The patron now has what all other patrons have, a ticket stub, with the date and seat location on it. Should there be reason for exchange or refund, the ticket is still identified as SPT by the rubber stamp on the back.

This method provides security for the box office, as there is clear proof of each SPT sold. It provides security for the theatre operator as well, as the resale for full price of half a ticket with a coupon stuck to it is much more difficult. Is it worth the effort? Only your local conditions can help you determine what is necessary. A careful examination of the problems and questions each theatre operator wants to resolve will determine exactly what methods the theatre should use in its discount ticket system.

A final note: anytime a ticket is returned to the box office for exchange or refund—which will happen despite all the announcements and rules, or as the result of a canceled performance, the ticket seller must make it a habit to look at the back of every ticket, and make sure that only that which was paid, is credited to the customer. Refunding more than you took in can lead to disaster.

Special Patron Ticket Program

The _____ Theatre makes available a limited number of half-priced tickets to those of limited income. This program receives no government funding and is only possible through the cooperation of the visiting attractions.

Discounted tickets are available as follows:

Children through high school age may each purchase one ticket. No school ID is required, but children must be present at the time of purchase to receive a discount ticket.

College and graduate students (full time, currently enrolled) may purchase two tickets with a valid student ID.

Citizens with a limited income may purchase two tickets with a human resources card.

Disabled persons may purchase two tickets.

Senior citizens sixty-five and older may purchase two tickets.

These Special Patron Tickets are available for weekday performances. However, a limited number of half-priced tickets for disabled persons are available for all performances.

Special Patron Tickets may be purchased for any seating area of the theatre. Since the number of tickets available under this program is limited, it is possible for Special Patron Tickets to sell out, while regular full-price tickets are still available.

These Special Patron Tickets are not transferable and, like all theatre tickets, may not be exchanged or refunded.

To purchase these discount tickets, eligible persons must:

1. Come in person to the theatre during box office hours

2. Before going to the box office window, obtain a validated SPT coupon from the theatre office by presenting a valid I.D.

3. Take the coupon(s) to the box office to purchase the ticket(s).

4. Disabled patrons may order SPT tickets by phone by calling _____.

Memorandum

To: Special price ticket monitors
Subject: Instructions for validating SPT coupons

1. Have patron fill out coupon for each ticket to be purchased.

2. Check student ID for each coupon. Note eligibility limits.

3. Any validated coupons that are not used are to be destroyed.

4. Do not assist any theatre employee who calls or otherwise requests you to give them validated coupons. Direct their requests to the theatre manager.

Form 1–25

SPT

☐ Student

☐ Senior Citizen

☐ _____

Date:

Form 1-26

SPECIAL PATRON TICKET	SPT
Attraction_____Date_____	☐ Student
	☐ Senior Citizen
☐ Student ☐ Senior Citizen ☐ _____	☐ _____
Patron Name_____	Date:

Form 1–27

GROUP SALES

A large theatre booked a children's show, hoping to attract students and children's organizations. Through extensive homework and legwork, the group sales person began to take orders for tickets. Eventually, sales from individual school classes, scout groups, and other clubs reached acceptable levels, even with the students' discount. That was good, because single ticket sales were negligible. Then the local public school system got interested. Recognizing that the show was indeed a good one for students, the system ordered literally thousands of tickets.

The next day, the cancellations started coming in from the scout groups and individual classes. Virtually every order the theatre had made by itself was canceled. At least it was a wash, thought the theatre folk. But some governments are not real quick to pay their bills and debts, so as the performances came and went—attended by all those school kids—but there was no money in hand.

Then the other shoe fell. The powers that be determined that the order for all those tickets was not properly done, not in compliance with official policies and procedures, and the purchase orders were invalid. Result: no payment. Gross receipts: virtually zero.

Just think of the efficiency. You know how hard it is to sell one pair of tickets. Imagine how great it would be to sell, with only a little more effort, fifty tickets. But note that selling tickets to a group is different, because the problems of a group are often different from those of an individual ticket holder.

If events occur that make the holder of one or two tickets unhappy, you have many ways to deal with that problem. You can exchange the tickets, or give a refund, or even do nothing. The magnitude of the remedy is one you can probably live with. But multiply that by fifty, and you can see the dimensions of the problem. Exchange fifty tickets? Not possible. Refund fifty tickets? No way. Have fifty people swearing at you and bad mouthing your theatre all over town? You might as well go out of business.

The group's problems with tickets are not just bigger than an individual's, they are different. A group is often planning to resell their tickets, sometimes for more than they paid you, sometimes for less. As a consequence, the theatre's problems are also different.

The group might show up for a performance that is sold out, and the group has tickets for tomorrow's performance. What are you going to do with fifty very angry people hanging around your lobby? Or worse, what if their tickets were for last night?

The group may be planning a big fundraising event. They will buy your tickets, then resell them at a higher price, hoping to make lots of money. The group may be depending on that event to help it financially throughout the year. If something goes wrong, not only might the group lose the opportunity to make a big profit, it may not even have the money it needed to pay you for the tickets in the first place. Just cancel the order you say? What are you going to do with an extra fifty tickets dumped on you at the last minute?

Perhaps the group is not trying to make a lot of money, instead it is providing a social service for its members. Enabling the group members to buy tickets at less than box office price is great—until the group advertises and starts selling discount tickets to the public and undercutting the box office price.

To avoid these headaches you have to be organized, and do your paper work. You could just sell the group a lot of tickets, one by one, but that can be quite cumbersome, especially if they are discounted.

Overcoming the problems is well worth the effort. You should develop a long list of groups and organizations, because many will become repeat customers. Be nice to your groups. Encourage them. Keep them informed. Help them have successful events.

If a group is trying to decide whether or not to purchase tickets for a certain show, and they ask if that show is suitable for their group, be sure to give an honest answer. There are shows that are not suitable for children or church groups or senior citizens or schools that would be very sensitive to parental criticism. The theatre's credibility must be kept secure, and the confidence of the group leader must be maintained.

Groups often have to plan far in advance, sometimes many months or even a year before the performance date. When you are contacted before you have a firm schedule, be sure to record all necessary information about the inquiry—group, contacts, dates or shows desired, approximate number of seats, and so on. This information can easily be added to your mailing list, even if the first inquiry is the last (Form 1-28). After receiving the first inquiry, send the group a letter, and keep them up to date (Form 1-29).

Before agreeing on a specific date, the group seller must have accurate, up to the minute information on the availability of seats—date, time and price. Even if the group reserves seats before they go on sale to the public, there will be prior obligations, subscription, house, and so on. You cannot sell what you do not have and should not make promises the theatre cannot keep. Accordingly, do not promise specific locations before the tickets are pulled from the rack and set aside for the group. (This is done for a confirmed order, even before any payment has been received.)

When you and a group have finally decided on a specific performance and price, you must prepare a written contract. Whether it is a simple order form type agreement, Form 1-30, or a more detailed, fine print contract, Form 1-31, you must get it signed by the group leader.

Form 1-32 is a letter to send to the group leader with the contract the theatre has prepared. The contract should be prepared in several parts, with different colored or labeled parts. The number of parts you need will be determined by the amount of redundancy and security you need for your particular system. The variables include the following:

Group sales keeps one part, one part is sent to the box office to reserve the block of tickets. Two copies are mailed to the group. The group keeps one of those and mails one copy, now signed, back to the theatre. The signed copy is retained by the group sales office. When paid tickets are picked up at the box office, the group representative should show his/her copy of the contract to the ticket seller for identification. (You do not want someone walking away with a few thousand dollars of tickets without proper identification.) The box office matches that copy to the tickets that have already been set aside for the group. The contract is marked to indicate the specific ticket locations or numbers and the date the tickets are actually mailed or delivered to the group. After the performance involved, the box office contract is attached to the box office statement as back up for the discount and group sales commissions, if any. A group sold at full price does not appear anywhere on a performance statement (unless a commission is charged).

There are two items you must have in hand before any tickets are released to the group: a signed contract and money. The theatre must keep all the leverage. Never give out some of the tickets for partial payment. Chances are, you will never be paid for the unused tickets. Instead, insist on a deposit at the time a firm reservation is made. This is when a contract is signed and a commitment is made for the seats. Whenever possible, wait for a check to clear before you give out the tickets. Many groups are too optimistic about their own ability to sell seats.

A deadline must be set for payment in full. The cutoff should be far enough in advance of the performance so that if the order must be canceled, the tickets can still be sold. Only after you have been paid in full for the full value of the contract—that is all the tickets—should you transfer any of the tickets to the group. Never transfer any tickets before you have been paid for them. While the patron is at the window, make him or her count the entire stack of tickets right then.

When groups are given discounts, be sure to mark them by placing a rubber stamp on the back of every single ticket sold for that price. Both ends of the ticket must have the discount price stamped on it. This may require numerous rubber stamps for the variable prices you may have. Again, while there will be a stated policy of no refunds and no exchanges, there is always the possibility of exceptions and canceled performances. Of course, individual tickets from a group should not be exchanged or refunded.

Ticket markings should be different for the different sales and prices involved. The box office must always be able to identify instantly if a ticket was sold by group or subscription or otherwise, and exactly, to the penny, what the ticket was sold for.

If the theatre is busy, it may be desirable for the group sales director to prepare a daily and or weekly report of activity (Forms 1-33 and 1-34).

In some communities, some organizations can not come up with the cash in advance. Decisions you make about waiving any of the guidelines above should be made only with full awareness of the risks involved. Some groups may have trouble selling all their tickets, even though they have sold some of them. Any policy you want to establish regarding partial sales is your choice to make, but beware of letting groups dump large numbers of tickets back at the box office.

Date of Inquiry_____

Show: _____

Group: _____

Date of Performance: _____

# of Seats	Location	Price (Discount)	Total

Payment due by _____   Total _____

                                    Deposit_____ Due _____

                                    Balance_____ Due _____

Name _____

Address _____

_____

_____

Phone _____

Form 1-28

Dear Group Leader:

Thank you for your inquiry.

 Scheduling has not been completed for the time period you have requested, but please be assured that we will keep your letter on file and send you complete information as soon as it becomes available.

 Your name has also been placed on our group mailing list and you will receive all further information on productions of this theatre.

Sincerely,

_____

Group Sales Director

Form 1-29

Group Sales Agreement

Show _____ Performance Date _____

Organization _____ Telephone _____

Address   _____

Contact   _____ Telephone _____

#_____ $_____ tickets sold at $_____   Total: $_____

#_____ $_____ tickets sold at $_____   Total: $_____

Amount due box office: $_____

Less deposit received: ($_____)

Balance due box office: $_____

Date ordered _____ Date balance due _____

1. No tickets will be transferred to Organization until all tickets are paid in full.

2. If for any reason the performance is not given, after Organization's tickets are returned to box office, Theatre will refund to Organization price paid for the tickets. Organization will make no other claim for damages or other compensation.

3. If balance due Box Office is not paid by due date, this agreement will be canceled and all money paid will be retained by Theatre as liquidated damages.

4. Organization will not sell tickets to anyone but the ultimate user, nor advertise to public tickets at less than full box office price.

_____ To be picked up.   Paid in full _____

_____ To be mailed.   Cannot fill _____

_____ Holding order.   Date mailed _____

Notes

Theatre_____ Organization_____

Tickets received by _____ Date _____

Form 1-30

Group Sales Contract

Attraction:_____

Performance date:_____ m/e_____p.m.

This Agreement is entered into this ___ day of _____, 19__, by and between
_____ (Theatre)
and _____ (Buyer).

The parties agree to the following:

1. The Theatre agrees to sell to the Buyer and the Buyer agrees to purchase from the Theatre tickets entitling the Buyer to occupy the seats listed below for the performance of the attraction identified above, to be performed at the day and time shown above.

Total number of tickets:_____ Total price:_____
The Buyer agrees to pay for the tickets as follows:

a. 25% of the total price upon signing of this Agreement ($_____).

b. Before delivery of the tickets, the balance of the total price ($_____).

2. Upon payment in full of the total price, the Theatre agrees to make the tickets available for distribution to the Buyer at least _____days/weeks prior to the day of the performance.

    If the Buyer fails to make any payments required, then at the Theatre's option, the Buyer will return to Theatre any tickets it has received for a refund, or Theatre will retain any money already paid by Buyer as liquidated damages, in addition to any other rights and remedies the Theatre may have.

3. The Buyer will pay any special or extra costs incurred for the printing of special tickets.

4. If tickets are sold to Buyer at a discount or at less than regular box office price, then Buyer agrees:

a. Buyer will not advertise in any manner to the public, tickets for sale at a price below the regular box office price, without the Theatre's written consent.

b. Buyer will not sell, trade or give any tickets to any ticket broker, agency, or any party other than the ultimate user of such tickets.

5. At Theatre's option, the Theatre will accept from Buyer unsold tickets, and place them at the box office for sale to the public at regular box office prices. Proceeds from any such sale shall be for the credit of the Buyer, except that where Buyer has purchased tickets under this Agreement for less than regular box office price, then Theatre shall credit Buyer only the amount paid by Buyer, and Theatre shall retain the difference

—(more)—

between the Buyer's cost and the price received by Theatre at the box office. Where Buyer's tickets are sold at the box office for less that Buyer's cost (e.g. SPT program), then Buyer shall be credited only for the amount received by the box office. All such credits shall be computed on the basis of net receipts.

Theatre shall have no obligation to sell any or all of Buyer's tickets, nor shall Theatre be obligated to attempt to sell Buyer's tickets before other tickets are sold at the box office, regardless of date or time.

6. If for any reason the performance is not presented, and the Theatre and Buyer are not able to agree on a different performance, the Theatre will refund to Buyer money paid to Theatre, after all tickets issued to Buyer have been returned to Theatre. Thereafter, neither party shall have any obligation or liability to the other.

   The Buyer acknowledges that the Theatre cannot guarantee the artistic nature of the performance, and that the nature of the performance is subject to change by the attraction.

7. Tickets are sold subject to availability of location, and shall be selected by Theatre in its sole discretion. Locations are subject to change as required by the attraction. The Theatre shall have the right to withhold seats for special use, but without cost to Buyer.

8. This Agreement contains the entire agreement of the parties, and no alterations or amendments shall exist unless in writing and signed by both parties.

For the _____ Theatre: For the Buyer:

_____   _____

_____   _____

_____   _____

Form 1–31

Dear Group Leader:

It is a pleasure to confirm your request for tickets. Please sign and return the original/white copy of the enclosed contract, along with your check made payable to the _____ Theatre. Full payment is needed by the due date indicated on the contract. Five days after we receive your final check, you may pick up the tickets at the theatre. Please bring the blue copy of the contract with you at that time. If you prefer, we will send the tickets to you by certified mail. Please enclose an extra two dollars for postage and handling.

Please mail the white copy of the contract and your check to:

                    _____ Theatre
                    Group Sales Office
                    xxxxxxxxxxxxxxxxx,
                    xxxxxxxxxxx, xx   xxxxx

If we are unable to mail your tickets, they will be held for you at the box office.

Your interest and patronage of the _____ theatre is greatly appreciated. We hope your group enjoys the performance and that we can be can be of service to you again in the future.

Form 1–32

GROUP SALES

SHOW_____

Date	Group Total	Paid Unpaid	New Contracts	Paid Today	Cancellations

Form 1-33

The Well-Run Theatre

Attraction_____ As of_____

	Total w/e	Total to Date
No. New Orders	_____	_____
$ New Orders	_____	_____
$ Canceled Orders	_____	_____
Subtotal	_____	_____
Played Off	_____	_____
Balance Advance	_____	_____
Paid Groups	_____	_____
Balance Due	_____	_____

Form 1--34

COUNTING TICKET STUBS

After each performance begins, someone must count and analyze the actual ticket stubs of people who are attending the performance. Instructions are on Form 1-35.

If any category of stub count is higher than the box office statement count, something is wrong. For example, if the box office says it sold fifty tickets at full price, and the drop has fifty-two tickets, there is a mistake that must be clarified. Is another category wrong? Perhaps the box office also reports it gave out four comps, but only two appeared in the drop. Check the exact ticket numbers or seat locations. Possibly the two missing comps were not properly marked, and they looked like full price tickets. Mystery solved. Or check for wrong date performances, or switched matinee and evening performances.

Too few tickets in the drop can signal other types of problems. For example, one hundred full price sales are reported, but only ninety stubs appear in the drop. Are there empty seats in the house? Are the ten people using some kind of coupon or other substitute for tickets? Are the ticket takers not really taking the tickets? Some of these answers may suggest that someone is cheating you.

Or was the weather bad?

Are there about 100 tickets missing? Maybe the box office has misplaced a bundle of 100 tickets, and has reported them sold at full price. Or maybe a large number of no shows are concentrated in a group sale, and it turns out the bus broke down on the way to the theatre. A quick way to check for a missing group is to just look at the house. As most group tickets are close together, a clump of empty seats usually indicates a group did not show up. Or did the group cancel its contract, and the box office forgot to release the tickets to be sold?

Sometimes you may need to count the number of people attending the performance. Are there more people in the house than expected by both the box office statement and the stub count? If some people did not have their tickets torn by the ticket takers, how did they get in? Are they actually holding tickets for that performance? Did they give their whole ticket to the ticket taker, who did not tear it but kept it? Did the ticket taker then give the ticket back to the ticket seller, who used it as deadwood to show it was never sold, and can thereby keep the money for himself? If you suspect any answers to these questions are yes, you may have a personnel problem. Or perhaps several members of the cast are sitting in the theatre watching the show until they have to go on. Or perhaps people from the balcony have sneaked into the orchestra.

Obviously there are many possible explanations for variations between the number of tickets reported sold, the number of tickets reported by the ticket takers, and the number of people in the house. There will always be a few no shows, the manager and box office treasurer will eventually be able to observe what is normal for their theatre, or for certain types of shows. It is the aberrations that must always be looked into.

Memorandum

To: Ushers
Subject: Counting ticket stubs

1. Sort all tickets by each full and discount price.

2. Stack tickets face up and in one direction, so that dates can be easily read by flipping the edge of the stack.

3. For each price range, make a separate stack of tickets that have been altered. Tickets stamped "Special Price Ticket", punched with a hole, or having a subscription mark should be counted separately.

4. Pile tickets into groups of 100, maximum. Write the number of tickets on the bottom of each stack. Bind the stack tightly with a rubber band.

5. Blue slips (SPT coupons) should be counted and recorded in the SPT column.

6. Fill out the ticket count sheet entirely, place all stubs and paper work in a bag, and give everything to the manager.

Form 1–35

The Well-Run Theatre

TICKET TAKER'S STUB COUNT

Attraction _____ Day _____ mat ___ eve ___

Performance No. _____ Date _____

	Full Price	Group	SPT	Comp	Sub	Total	Price Scale
Front Orch	_____	_____	_____	_____	_____	_____	_____
Rear Orch	_____	_____	_____	_____	_____	_____	_____
Balc	_____	_____	_____	_____	_____	_____	_____
Total	_____	_____	_____	_____	_____	_____	_____

LOST TICKET CARDS: No. of seats:
    (Number of cards:_____)   _____

                                                GRAND
                                       _____ TOTAL

Weather:_____

_____
Signature of Counter

Memorandum

To: Box office treasurer
Subject: The performance package

Box Office statements for all scheduled performances—whether given or not—together with the following materials must be delivered to the manager's office no later than the start of business on the next regular business day after the performance.

1. The box office statement.

2. Complimentary ticket orders (and summary list), properly authorized.

3. All deadwood.

4. All ticket stubs with stub count sheet, including lost ticket locations.

5. All documentation authorizing reductions in price (including subscription statements, special price tickets, group discounts, etc.).

6. All documents on which commissions or fees deducted from the statement are based (credit card charges, vendor fees, etc.).

7. All documentation not already included above representing sales reported on the statement not yet paid to the box office (such as guaranteed tickets not picked up, etc.).

8. Audit stubs.

Form 1–37

The Well-Run Theatre

BOX OFFICE STATEMENT

Day_____ Date _____

Weather_____ ☐ Mat. ☐ Eve. at _____

Attraction_____ Performance No._____ Week No. _____

LOCATION	CAPACITY	DEAD WOOD	COMPS	SPECIAL RATES	TOTAL UNSOLD	SOLD	PRICE		AMOUNT	
Orch A-G	150	8	2	50	60	90	6	00	540	00
H-T	100	46	0	0	46	54	5	00	270	00
Balcony	150	34	0	23	57	93	4	00	372	00
TOTALS	400	88	2	73	163	237			1182	00

HARDWOOD		OPENING NUMBER	CLOSING NUMBER		

SPECIAL RATES	REG. PRICE	%			SOLD	PRICE		AMOUNT		
Group	6.00	20%			50	4	80	240	00	
	4.00	20%			23	3	20	73	60	
TOTALS					73	313	60	313	60	

We hereby certify that the undersigned have personally checked the above statement and it is in every way correct.

SUBTOTAL	1495	60
5% Group	⟨15	68⟩
5% Credit Card	⟨23	17⟩
NET THIS PERF.	1456	75
PREV. TOTAL	1206	00
TOTAL TO DATE	2662	75

BOX OFFICE TREASURER _____

THEATRE MANAGER _____

COMPANY MANAGER

SEAT ORDER

Attraction

Ordered By

For

No. & Location   2 orch.   C101, 102

Day & Date   Sat   4-7-90   Mat (Eve)

No.   2   x $ 6.00   = Total Due   N/C

If not called for, release by:

☐ 24 Hours   ☐ 6PM (noon)   ☐ Guaranteed

Authorized By

Kindly sign below to acknowledge receipt of tickets.

Form 1-39

Group Sales Agreement

Show _____ Performance Date _____

Organization _____ Telephone _____

Address _____

Contact _____ Telephone _____

#_ 50 _ $_ 6.00 _ tickets sold at $_ 4.80 _   Total: $_ 240.00 _

#_ 23 _ $_ 4.00 _ tickets sold at $_ 3.20 _   Total: $_ 73.60 _

Amount due box office: $ 313.60

20% Less deposit received: ($ 62.72)

Balance due box office: $ 250.88

Date ordered _ 6-1-92 _   Date balance due _ 7-1-92 _

1. No tickets will be transferred to Organization until all tickets are paid in full.

2. If for any reason the performance is not given, after Organization's tickets are returned to box office, Theatre will refund to Organization price paid for the tickets. Organization will make no other claim for damages or other compensation.

3. If balance due Box Office is not paid by due date, this agreement will be canceled and any monies paid will be retained by Theatre as liquidated damages.

4. Organization will not sell tickets to anyone but the ultimate user, nor advertise to public tickets at less than box office price.

____✓____ To be picked up.   Paid in full _____

_____ To be mailed.   Cannot fill _____

_____ Holding order.   Date mailed _____

Notes

Theatre_____ Organization_____

Tickets received by _____ Date _____

TICKET TAKER'S STUB COUNT

Attraction   Day   mat   eve

Performance No.   Date

	Full Price	Group	SPT	Comp	Sub	Total	Price Scale
Front Orch	82	49		2		133	6.00
Rear Orch	54					54	5.00
Balc	90	23				113	4.00
Total	226	72		2		300	

LOST TICKET CARDS: No. of seats: 0
        (Number of cards:_____)

                                         300   **GRAND TOTAL**

Weather: _Cold + Rain_

_____
Signature of Counter

AUDIENCE STATISTICS

Show_____ w/e_____

	Number	$ Amount
Deadwood		
Regular		
Students		
Senior		
Groups		
Standing Room		
Complimentary		
Total Sales		
Net Gross Receipts		

Form 1–42

ANNUAL AUDIENCE STATISTICS

Regardless of the type of box office system you run, management should keep regular statistics on the number and type of tickets sold. This is essential to prove to your community how wonderful your organization is, and what successful outreach programs you have, and how you are always encouraging new audiences to attend performing arts. If you keep track of this information weekly, then compiling annual statistics is very easy. At the end of the year, just add up the weekly reports and convert the date line to the year.

Memorandum

To: Box office treasurer
Subject: Box office audit

After the box office closes on Saturday, August 31st, an audit will be conducted of all box office business transacted through that date.

Please schedule your staff so that all personnel necessary for the audit will be available. The audit will continue until completed, which may take most of the night. Please note much of the work can, and should be, completed in advance.

1. Your checkbook, up to date, with current balances reconciled with the bookkeeper. Deposits should be prepared through that day's business, and all checks for completed performances issued. No checks or deposits should be dated after August 31.

2. For performances given, be certain that all amounts due from other sources are paid or accounted for. This must include agencies, ticket brokers, computer services, telephone charges, paid groups, theatre petty cash IOUs, and all other sources.

3. All amounts payable from box office but not yet paid should be listed. This includes individual refunds, performances canceled but not yet fully refunded, credit slips issued but not redeemed, unused gift certificates, and amounts due the manager's account. All claims should be fully supported with appropriate documentation.

4. Documents supporting any tickets sold for a discount for future performances.

5. Any tickets not in box office are reported as sold. Any seat orders for complimentary tickets must be available. Seat orders for tickets to be (but not yet) paid must be available.

6. Box office statements for all future performances should be prepared in advance, including actual count of all deadwood as of August 31st. All tickets will be recounted at time of audit.

Form 1–43

Memorandum

To: Box office treasurer
Subject: Standard box office procedures

As part of our upcoming audit of box office operations, please confirm that the following items are all performed or accounted for as necessary.

Yes No

___ ___ Actual number of seats identical to ticket printer's manifest

___ ___ Actual number of tickets identical to ticket printer's manifest

___ ___ Any changes in seating capacity reflected on box office statements

___ ___ All standing room tickets properly accounted for

___ ___ Full price group tickets properly marked

___ ___ Discount group tickets properly marked with actual price

___ ___ Complimentary tickets properly marked

___ ___ Subscription tickets properly identified with actual price

___ ___ All unsold tickets counted by two people for each performance

___ ___ Actual ticket prices correctly shown on box office statements

___ ___ Group discount contracts attached and checked for each performance

___ ___ Group discounts correctly accounted for on box office statements

___ ___ Complimentary ticket documents properly prepared and attached to statement for each performance

___ ___ Agency commissions correctly deducted from each box office statement

___ ___ Credit card agency commissions correctly deducted from each box office statement

___ ___ Subscription commissions correctly deducted from box office statements

___ ___ All arithmetic double checked on box office statements

___ ___ Previous total receipts brought forward correctly

—(more)—

___ ___ No obvious problems during sellout (e.g. double sold locations, no tickets sold for non-existent seats, no seats left empty)

___ ___ Group tickets returned to theatre correctly accounted for

___ ___ Ticket takers' stub counts compared to box office statement

___ ___ Petty cash and other IOUs properly and promptly repaid

___ ___ Bank deposits made every day

___ ___ Transfer to manager's account for the correct amounts for each attraction

___ ___ Box office account opening balance properly accounted for

___ ___ Box office checking account regularly reconciled, accounting for checks and deposits in transit

Form 1–44

Audit Report

Date:_____

Instructions: This form is to be completed during the proceeding of the box office audit. If an item does not apply, indicate "n/a," do not leave any printed lines blank. Box office treasurer, theatre manager, and auditor must sign below before exiting the box office.

ASSETS:

Check book balance   _____

Cash on hand   _____

Deposits in transit   _____

IOUs   _____

Due from telephone charge   _____

Due from credit cards   _____

Due from credit certificates   _____

Due from subscription   _____

Due from groups   _____

Due from agencies   _____

—(more)—

The Well-Run Theatre

Paid gift certificates _____

Unsold tix for future perfs. _____

Uncollected guarantees _____

Due from Manager _____

Total Assets: ==================

LIABILITIES:

Group commissions _____

Canceled performances _____

Credit certificates _____

Gift certificates _____

Due to Manager _____

Consignments _____

Future performances _____

Total Liabilities: ==================

Total Assets: _____

Total Liabilities: _____

Surplus (Shortage): ==================

Average per week since last audit: _____

Prepared by:

_____
Auditor

_____
Box Office Treasurer

_____
Theatre Manager

Form 1–45

Chapter 2
Visiting Attractions

The process of booking an attraction involves two distinct, yet inseparable actions. The first is finding an attraction and coming to a tentative agreement that that attraction, playing at your theatre, is a good idea. The second element is negotiating the financial arrangement involved with the attraction playing at the theatre. It may be that an attraction simply costs too much to present in your theatre, because your theatre does not have enough seats. That is, even if the show were to sell out at the high end of your ticket scales, either the attraction, or the theatre, will lose money. There may be no way to split the box office receipts so that both parties are financially secure. This applies even if the theatre or attraction has third party funding (e.g. grants or contributions). Of course, some organizations are not solely dependent on box office receipts. Nevertheless, all organizations have some budget, and whatever the source of their revenue, they must at least break even.

The Attraction List (Form 2–1), is designed as a handy weekly guide to the staff of upcoming major events. It does not list every event taking place in the facility, only those that will be tying up most of the theatre space and the staff's time. It is a handy aid for the booker as it easily shows gaps in the schedule. Frequently updated, the list can be regularly circulated to the staff.

The Booking Request (Form 2–2), is just a preliminary note for the person responsible for scheduling attractions in the theatre. When properly filled out, it provides minimum information necessary when a first inquiry is made for a show. The information shown might not be the final dates or terms eventually agreed to. The form's use is not limited to outside attractions, and can be used for in house productions as well. The form indicates special details and exceptions to the performance schedule and price scale.

Because theatres get frequent requests for information on the facilities available, a sample theatre information sheet is provided (Form 2–3). It is also a good idea to send the attraction a copy of your seating chart, floor plans, and stage drawings. Similarly, the theatre manager or stage manager needs to know in advance what equipment the attraction will bring with it or needs to use at the theatre, so an attraction inquiry form is shown (Form 2-4).

The Application to Use Theatre and information for applicants (Form 2-5) was developed for use in a municipal auditorium, where the local government is involved, and government funds support the institution. The scale of rates is shown only to indicate one pattern of assessing costs.

Attractions	
	Today's date_____
4/21 - 4/27	
4/28 - 5/4	
5/5 - 5/11	
5/12 -5/18	
5/19 -5/25	
5/26 - 6/1	
6/2 - 6/8	
6/9 - 6/15	
6/16 - 6/22	
6/23 - 6/29	
6/30 - 7/6	
7/7 - 7/13	
7/14 - 7/20	
7/21 - 7/27	
7/28 - 8/3	
8/4 - 8/10	
8/11 - 8/17	
8/18 - 8/24	
8/25 - 8/31	
9/1 - 9/7	
9/8 - 9/14	
9/15 - 9/21	
9/22 - 9/28	
9/29 - 10/5	

Form 2–1

Booking Request

Dates Required:_____

Attraction:_____

Producer/Promoter:_____

Address/Phone:_____

Stars/Author:_____

Terms or Rental requested:_____

_____

_____

Schedule:_____

    Omissions:_____

Price Scale:_____

Date of first inquiry:_____

Form 2–2

Theatre Information

Address:

Seating Capacity:
Orchestra: 250
Balcony: <u>150</u>
400

Scenery Load In:
At stage right, enter loading alley from right side of theatre. Loading dock at stage level, under cover, straight line to stage. Dollies and hand carts available.

Dressing Rooms:
All off stage right, each room has one sink. All rooms contain at least one sink, wardrobe rack, shower stall, lighted counter.

1st floor: two Star rooms, each with private toilet and sink, one has private shower.

2nd floor: eight rooms, each designed for two people.

3rd floor: four rooms, each for four people.

4th floor: four rooms, each for four people.

Wardrobe:
In basement under dressing rooms, washer, dryer, large sink, iron, ironing board, and work room available.

Rehearsal Room:
Lower level of dressing room area.

Stage Dimensions:
Proscenium Opening: (maximum)
Width: 32'8"
Height: 18' 7/16"
Curtain line to upstage wall: 34'4"
Left wall to right wall: 68'6"
Offstage, left and right: 18'0"

Height of grid: 62'0"
Length of pipe: 42'0"
Number of working sets: 48

Stage Floor:
Masonite, dark brown, no paint or wax. Entire on-stage area trapable. Dance floor available.

House curtain:
Drop, center opening, no side access when in, manually operated.

Electrics:
Available power: Nine 400 amp legs, boards plug in stage left. All cable must pass 50 mega-ohms resistance. Balcony rail, ceiling access, box booms at side of balcony. House has full complement of light and controllers.

—(more)—

Sound: Road consoles usually locate behind orchestra seats,
                          house right.
                          House has full complement of house sound control
                          and speakers.

Orchestra Pit: Capacity about 25 players. Can be raised to
                          orchestra floor level or stage level, and can be
                          covered to match stage floor. Music stands with lights
                          available.

Scenery: Must be fireproofed to local standards; New York
                          scene shop certificates have no importance if scenery
                          holds a flame. City fire department will inspect and
                          test scenery. Many shows must refireproof at the
                          theatre.

Contacts: [include names, addresses, and telephone numbers,
                          as appropriate]

General Management
General Manager
Theatre Manager
Box Office Treasurer
Public Relations
Group Sales
Subscription
Public Telephone number
Visiting staff phone
Concessionaire
Head Usher
Telephone sales (public)
Program Publisher
Bank
House Doctor
Advertising Representative
Post Office
Taxis
Stage Doorman
Dressing room pay phone number
Head Carpenter
Head Electrician
Head Property man & Steward
Wardrobe
Musical Contractor

Form 2–3

Attraction Information

Note: Always provide names, addresses and phone numbers.

Attraction:

_____

Dates of performances:

_____

Producer:

_____

Technical Director:

_____

Stage Manager:

_____

Scenery Designer:

_____

Lighting Designer:

_____

Road Crew Heads:

    Carpenter:

    Electrician:

    Property:

_____

Orchestra Leader:

_____

Number of performers:

_____

Number of dressing rooms needed:

_____

—(more)—

Is this a Yellow Card Show?

	Spot Lines	In	Show	Out
Carpenter				
Electric				
Property				
Wardrobe				

Take In: Date_____ Time_____

    Arriving from_____ Est. hours to take in_____

    Number of trucks_____

Take out: Date_____ Time_____

    Destination_____ Est. hours to take out_____

Number of loaders needed

Show: Number of intermissions_____ Running time_____

Musicians: Number needed _____ Attach orchestrations.

Rehearsal space needs:

Attach full details for equipment needed from theatre.

Form 2–4

Application to Use Theatre

Applications may be submitted up to one year in advance of the first performance date. As of June 1st of each year, the City will prepare a schedule for the upcoming season. Applications may also be submitted any time in advance of the event, with all parties acknowledging that a short lead time will significantly affect the availability of dates and the ability of the parties to prepare for the event.

Applications for the use of the theatre are accepted in accordance with the priority list determined by the City. However, for artistic or other reasons, the City reserves the right to allow exceptions to the established list. As a general rule, the intention of the City is to provide for constant use of the facility. Consequently, weekends or excessive time will seldom be provided for preparation work, rehearsals, or other non-public events.

Application fees of $_____ are required for the first application from one applicant, and $_____ for all additional applications from the same applicant for engagements in the same season. Accepted organizations may apply the application fee to its costs. Applications that are denied will have the fee returned to the applicants.

_____ percent (_____%) of the expected total fees and costs must be paid at the time the signed booking agreement is returned to the theatre.

If less than _____ percent (_____%) of the potential gross box office receipts are to be sold by the theatre box office, then the balance of the total fees and costs must be paid to theatre in advance of the first performance.

If any payments to theatre are not made according to the schedule set forth in the agreement, the event is subject to cancellation and all money previously paid to theatre will be forfeited to theatre as liquidated damages.

Standard Priority Order:

1. Not for profit performing arts organizations located in _____ City.
2. Commercial performing arts organizations or individuals located in _____ City.
3. Not for profit performing arts organizations based outside _____ City.
4. Commercial performing arts organizations or individuals based outside _____ City.
5. Other not for profit organizations located in _____ City.
6. Other commercial organizations or individuals based outside _____ City.

Fees and Costs for Use of Community Theatre

SPACE
Theatre (includes stage, auditorium,
    dressing rooms, lobbies, and
    box office services) $_____
Auditorium Only $_____
Stage Only $_____
Rehearsal Room $_____
Lobby/Reception areas Only $_____
EQUIPMENT
Theatre lighting system $_____
Theatre sound system $_____
Dance floor - installation (in & out) $_____
Dance floor - per day installed $_____
Piano $_____
Piano tunings $_____

—(more)—

PERSONNEL
Additional tech crew $_____
Additional box office $_____
Additional cleaning $_____

Supplies, materials, etc. shall be charged as incurred.

Not for profit performing arts organizations shall receive a discount of _____ (_____%) off the above listed costs.

Application to Use Theatre

Name of organization   _____

    Contact: _____

    Address: _____

                            _____

    Telephone: day_____eve_____Fax_____

Is this organization a not for profit organization in this state?_____

If your organization submits more than one application, list your priority number of this application here_____

Type of event (Theatre, dance, concert, etc.)_____

Number of personnel: On stage_____ Back stage_____ Off stage_____

Dates Requested:	Date	Time	Fee
Take in Scenery	_____	_____	_____
Rehearsals	_____	_____	_____
	_____	_____	_____
Performances	_____	_____	_____
	_____	_____	_____
	_____	_____	_____
Take out	_____	_____	_____

TOTAL RENTAL FEES: _____

Signature_____

—(more)—

71

The Well-Run Theatre

For office use only:

Date application submitted _____

Deposit received_____ Amount_____

Dates locked in on _____

Booking agreement sent to organization on _____

Signed agreement due no later than _____

Signed agreement received on _____

Form 2-5

CONTRACTS BETWEEN THE THEATRE AND THE ATTRACTION

Having agreed with the representative of the attraction on the basic theory of dividing the financial receipts and liabilities, a written agreement must be drawn.

The theatre operator must have a written agreement with every attraction that will perform in his theatre. This agreement need not be elaborate or technical, but it needs to exist. Anything can go wrong when presenting performing arts. Difficulties arise regardless of how well the parties know each other, or what understanding they believe they have between themselves. A cancelled performance, a snowstorm that wipes out all ticket sales, or a fire backstage are problems that can and do happen to theatres. When no money is coming in, determining who will suffer the financial loss becomes an enormous issue.

Procedural questions as well as major problems must be anticipated. Who will pay for the advertising? Who will print the programs? May the attraction sell its own souvenirs in the lobby during intermission? May the attraction sell candy, or may only the theatre do that? Who will get the liquor license? Who will pay for the extra electric cable that had to be rented because the theatre did not have enough available for the show? There is no end to the possibilities. Some questions are easily resolved, some are not. If the questions have been anticipated in a well-written agreement, there might be frustration or unhappiness, but not argument.

Nevertheless, while a Broadway producer may expect to sign a five- or ten-page contract with lots of fine print, a small community acting company may be totally intimidated by such a document. The parties will have to decide how detailed and specific they want to be. It certainly does not make sense to pay the lawyers more to prepare and explain an agreement than the show can possibly gross.

The sample contracts in this chapter are arranged in order of complexity, beginning with the simplest. Operators should examine all the samples, and consider what problems are addressed in each paragraph of each contract. By carefully picking and choosing relevant language, a manager can serve the needs of both his own operation, and those of the visiting attraction. Assemble relevant parts, and you have one or more standard agreements tailor made for your operation. Most operations will need to have more than one standard form available.

Note: many of the specific clauses in these samples are based on local laws and conditions. When considering language for insurance, for example, do not assume the language shown here can apply to your organization exactly as written. Consult your insurance carrier. Make sure your contract conforms to local building codes and fire regulations. Consult with your local fire department, or architect, or building contractor. Consult with your accountants and lawyers when creating your standard forms. Get competent professional advice in advance. After the form is written, only the negotiated *terms* are at issue with the other side, not the legalities.

Some notes regarding all contracts.

1. A multi-million dollar production may perform for weeks or months in a major theatre and never have a signed contract. When this situation arises, it usually occurs between a theatre operator and a producer who know each other personally, and both know what is expected of them in the industry. Further, the contract may never be signed because of some relatively minor disagreement in the fine print—reflecting a contingency that rarely arises—or a disagreement on allocation of cer-

tain expenses. In these situations, the problems either resolve themselves by becoming moot, or by waiting until the box office results are apparent and the parties are in a better position to determine the actual effects of their decisions. Because the professional theatre industry is so small, with few major producers and few major theatres, parties must do business with each other again and again. It serves neither party to try to stiff the other. They will resolve their problems in a professional manner, knowing that if this production is not successful, then perhaps the next one will be.

Operators of smaller theatres may also know their counterparts producing the shows they present, however, one or the other parties may be less familiar with what is common in the industry, and what is expected. A misunderstanding can be disastrous to any performing arts administrator. The hard feelings resulting when a theatre or company manager believes he was somehow cheated can cause lasting repercussions far beyond the walls of a theatre.

2. Be sure to get the name, address, and telephone numbers of the principle parties written right on the contract. You might know them now, but in a year or two this information may be buried in the theatre's files.

3. A theatre or producer will need to have more than one standard contract form available. The requirements of booking a week long acting company are different from booking a one night rock concert, or a once a month lecture series.

4. Negotiate your contract. These contract forms and samples should be used as guides, not taken word for word. The manager and producer must decide who will pay for each item, or provide which services. The parties must decide for themselves who will pay for the advertising, or who will pay for the lighting instruments. While the possibilities are endless, remember that bad deals can be made as easily as good ones.

5. "Do we need all this language?" is a fair question to ask. The answer of course, is that you will not know until after the show has closed and left the theatre, all checks have cleared the bank, and the statute of limitations has expired on contract law and personal injuries cases. The fine print contained in these sample contracts is like an insurance policy. The clauses are there in case you need them. If the theatre was not damaged by the attraction, the paragraphs on damage were not necessary. But if there is some damage, what can you do? The damage clauses set forth the party's obligations. The attraction may willingly pay for repairs; but if not, some legal remedy may be necessary. Naturally, a written contract is easier to enforce than an oral one.

Detailed language assigning in advance the rights and responsibilities of each party usually forces the parties to consider more carefully what they do. If the acting company knows it must restore the stage to the same condition as when they arrived in the theatre, the crew may be less likely to paint the stage floor so it looks like green grass.

Sometimes you merely want to put a producer on notice of some activity or policy in the theatre. For example, if you have a regular policy for discount tickets for students, say so in the contract. Otherwise, the theatre could end up liable to the producer for the lost income.

Form 2-6 is a specialty item. This theatre used a lobby for very small presentations, such as children's performers. This contract (it is a contract) does not include any of the topics the longer forms do. This is basically an information sheet, telling the small promoter some information needed to perform in the theatre's space. In this sample, the theatre is paying a fee to the attraction. Changing only a few words would have the attraction pay a fee to the theatre. If the attraction handles its own publicity and promotion, the paragraph requesting photographs may not be necessary.

Form 2-7 was designed for a small theatre renting the hall for a small concert, when the attraction will only be appearing for one performance. It is a simple letter between the theatre and the attraction, clearly identifying the basic responsibilities of each party. Some of the language is broadly stated, so as to be clear in its scope, such as "advertising, and everything necessary to present the performance at the Theatre." Other provisions are quite specific.

The Community Theatre Agreement, Form 2-8, was developed for a community or municipal theatre, where the local government is closely involved with its operation. Such a facility usually has regular technical crews, instead of union crews, and may be closely involved with the technical presentation of the attraction.

Form 2-9 is also used for a specific purpose, a regular lunchtime celebrity speaker program. In this situation, the promoter (attraction) is very limited in what he can do. Because the main stage is used when there is scenery from a regular show on it, there can be no refocusing lights, and no installation of scenery other than tables and chairs. This is a comprehensive agreement for the most basic use of a theatre, discussing many of the important topics, albeit briefly.

Form 2-10 was used by a community theatre, but it is based on a major theatre contract. It includes only those terms considered necessary by the local operator. Note the flexibility in the language. Paragraph 2 provides "the Theatre shall pay to Producer..." or "Producer shall pay to Theatre..."

Form 2-11 is a major contract, the type traditionally used by Broadway shows playing major theatres around the country. Much of the language is not needed by a community theatre, but is needed by a major theatre. Each clause should be reviewed and consideration given to the problems that clause tries to anticipate and solve.

Once you become familiar with the others, review Form 2-12. This type of contract is often made between a local promoter and the producer, not between the producer and a theatre operator. The promoter and the theatre must negotiate their own, separate agreement; which may take the form of one of the others shown in this chapter (e.g. Form 2-13). However, to simplify the relationships of the parties and to better illustrate their respective responsibilities, in this sample the parties are referred to as "Producer" and "Theatre."

This is a sample contract prepared from the *other* side, the producer's point of view. Note that a basic assumption underlying the contract is reversed. With house contracts (e.g. Form 2-11), the assumption is that if the contract does not say that the theatre will pay for something, then the show must pay for it. However, this show contract works the opposite way. If the contract does not state that the show pays for something, then the promoter (or theatre) must pay for it.

Note that nothing is left to chance. This contract is not just for a show that will play major professional theatres, but for theatres and auditoriums in smaller cities and towns. The producer cannot assume the personnel in those venues will be familiar with the needs of a major touring attraction. Consequently, every detail imaginable is spelled out explicitly. The local promoter is usually financially responsible for *everything* except the performers on stage. The promoter buys the show, the producer puts it on. The promoter pays a fee to the producer, the risk is entirely on the promoter. It is very strict, and the theatre/promoter is responsible for a great deal, all of which must be performed to the letter.

This contract is shown as a sample, not a model. The incredible detail included indicates that such an agreement must be substantially rewritten for each attraction the producer presents. Nevertheless, it is useful as a guide to what a promoter of some shows can expect to see.

Occasionally someone just wants to use your rehearsal room or stage to work on a show that is not playing at your theatre. Form 2-13 is a simple guide to renting that space.

Some theatres have lobby spaces than can be used for special events, private parties, cast parties, or outside rentals. Like everything else, the manager must keep track of the use of each space in his theatre. A Special Events Booking record is suggested.

Dear _____:

This is to confirm the agreement between _____ and the _____ Theatre for performances by your group at the "Saturday Morning" series of children's shows.

Your program will consist of _____. You will give two performances, each approximately fifty minutes long. The first performance will begin at 9:30 AM, the second performance will begin at 11:00 a.m.

The performances will be given in the theatre reception hall. The stage area is a carpeted, raised platform, 18" high, approximately 25 x 30 feet, not curtained. It has four standard 110 volt duplex electric outlets. A small storage area up stage may be used for dressing room or other purposes.

You have already seen and inspected the performance space.

You will be responsible for supplying all props, costumes, sound, and all other equipment necessary for your performance. The theatre has fixed, dimable lights.

You will arrive by 8:30 AM with your materials, while the audience will be admitted approximately twenty minutes before each performance. All your personnel and equipment must leave the theatre no later than 12:30 p.m.

The theatre will pay you $_____ for the two performances, payable immediately after the end of the second performance. There will be no admission charge to the audience.

You will send four 8" x 10" black and white photographs and one 8" x 10" color photograph for promotion and display.

You agree to indemnify and hold harmless the theatre from and against all actions, claims, suits, costs, liability, damages, or expenses of any kind that may be brought or made against the theatre or which the theatre must pay or incur by any reason of or resulting from injury, loss or damage to people or property resulting from the negligent performance or failure to perform any obligation under this agreement.

If the foregoing is agreeable to you, please sign below and return promptly.

Yours truly,

_____ Theatre

By: _____
        Title

Agreed to
By: _____

_____

_____

Form 2-6

Dear _____:

This letter will serve as our mutual agreement for the use and rental of the _____ Theatre.

The Theatre will be available to you for the setting up and performance of _____, on _____ (date), beginning at _____ (time), with a performance scheduled to begin at 8:00 PM. At the conclusion of the performance, you will have the theatre cleared and restored to its condition prior to your arrival.

You will pay to Theatre _____ dollars ($_____) at the time this signed agreement is returned to theatre. In consideration, the Theatre will permit you to retain one hundred percent (100%) of all money received from ticket sales for this one performance. Theatre capacity (standing room may not be sold) is _____.

You agree to provide adequate security in and about the theatre to ensure there will be no smoking, and no alcoholic beverages or illegal drugs of any kind used or distributed by anyone connected with the performance or in the audience.

You agree to provide your own tickets, advertising, and everything necessary to present the performance at the Theatre. You will also provide your own ticket seller and ticket taker.

The Theatre will provide the use of the box office, stage, and all public areas of the theatre. The Theatre will operate its regular concessions, and will retain all income therefrom.

The Theatre will permit you to use its light and sound equipment, under the strict supervision of the theatre's own crew. You may refocus lights, and need not restore to original focus after your performance.

Any performance licenses that may be required, such as B.M.I., ASCAP, or the like, shall be solely your responsibility.

The organization agrees to indemnify and hold harmless the Theatre from and against all actions, claims, suits, costs, liability, damages, or expenses of any kind which may be brought or made against the Theatre or which the Theatre must pay or incur by any reason of or resulting from injury, loss or damage to people or property resulting from the negligent performance or failure to perform any obligation under this agreement.

Your signature below confirms your agreement with the terms of this contract.

Theatre:

By:_____
                                                            Title

Attraction:

By:_____
                                                            Title

Community Theatre Booking Agreement

Name of organization _____

    Contact: _____

    Address: _____

                        _____

    Telephone: day _____ eve _____ Fax_____

Dates of use: (use additional sheets as necessary)

	Date	Time	Fee
Take in scenery	_____	_____	_____
Rehearsals	_____	_____	_____
	_____	_____	_____
Performances	_____	_____	_____
	_____	_____	_____
	_____	_____	_____
	_____	_____	_____
Take out	_____	_____	_____

Additional time or special clean up: _____

Extra services (see below)   _____

              Total Costs of Services: _____

Application fee paid   (_____)

Deposit paid   (_____)

    Balance of Amount due   _____

Extra services:

    Dance floor   _____

    Audio recording   _____

    Video recording   _____

    Piano   _____

    Piano tunings @_____   _____

    Extra tech crew   _____

    Extra box office   _____

    Reception room   _____

    Alcohol permit   _____

    Special insurance   _____

    Special security   _____

    _____   _____

    _____   _____

    _____   _____

    Total Extra Services   _____

—(more)—

General Information

1. The theatre manager shall determine fees for additional services or hours. The total number of hours will include time required from take in to clean up. Fees for extra services or materials, whether listed above or not, shall be promptly payable to theatre upon receipt of written notice to organization.

2. Any group remaining after the scheduled or reasonable time will be charged additional hours rent for any portion of an additional hour used.

3. No function will continue after 12:00 midnight. Exceptions may be arranged in advance with the Manager.

4. All fees are to be paid by check made payable to _____ City.

5. The organization will furnish the City, upon request, the following information:

    a. A copy of its articles of incorporation, and a certificate from IRS showing tax exempt status;
    b. A statement of the use to be made of the theatre;
    c. A certificate of insurance coverage during the term of use, indicating personal liability with a limit of $_____ per occurrence for bodily and property damage combined;
    d. Other information as required.

6. Bookings or any portion thereof canceled with less than four weeks written notice and that cannot be filled by another organization will result in the loss of the application fee and deposit called for in this agreement.

7. Should the theatre be destroyed or damaged to such an extent that such damage will substantially interfere with the use of the premises by the organization, this agreement shall terminate and the deposit will be refunded, less any costs already incurred by the theatre on behalf of the organization. The City agrees to refund all income from advance ticket sales for such canceled performances.

8. No collections, solicitations, or advertising shall be done on the premises without the written consent of the manager.

9. The City retains for itself all concession rights for sales and rentals, and all radio and television broadcasting, movie, film, video or audio tape, recording and transcription rights for any performances or events in the theatre unless expressly granted to the organization and outlined in an attachment to this agreement.

10. The consumption of alcoholic beverages is prohibited except to those groups authorized through exemption approved by the Manager, and in accordance with local regulations.

—(more)—

11.   An inspection of the premises shall be made before and after use to determine if damage to the theatre has resulted from any of the organizations' activities. Repairs shall be paid by organization.

12.   The organization assumes all costs arising from the use of copyrighted materials used in the performance. The organization assumes responsibility for payment of any dramatic or music licensing fees that may be required in connection with the events.

13.   This agreement cannot be assigned by organization, nor may the organization use the theatre in any way not specified in this agreement.

14.   The organization must abide by all applicable federal, state, and local laws and ordinances relevant to this agreement or the use of the theatre.

15.   In the event the organization is determined by the order of an appropriate agency or court to be in violation of nondiscrimination provisions of federal, state or local law, this agreement may be canceled, terminated or suspended in whole or in part by the City.

16.   The organization agrees to indemnify and hold harmless the City from and against all actions, claims, suits, costs, liability, damages, or expenses of any kind that may be brought or made against the City or which the City must pay or incur by any reason of or resulting from injury, loss or damage to people or property resulting from the negligent performance or failure to perform any obligation under this agreement.

17.   No term, provision or condition of this agreement may be altered or amended except upon the execution of a written agreement.

18.   Unless amended by this agreement, the organization is bound by all statements made in its application for use preceding this agreement. The reference to "organization" shall include all applicants, whether corporation, unincorporated association, an individual, or other type of user.

Organization:

_____
Signature

_____
Title

City:

_____
Signature

_____
Title

_____
Date

Lecture Agreement

In consideration of the mutual promises made herein, this agreement is entered into on _____, 19__, by the _____ Theatre Company, and_____, producer of _____ (Program), to take place on _____ (date).

1. The Theatre will provide at its expense the following services for the Program:

a. The auditorium, lobbies, and selected portions of the stage, from ____:____ AM until ____:____ PM on the day of the Program;

b. Lighting equipment sufficient to illuminate a speaker or small group of speakers on the stage. No focussing of lights will be possible, and no light cues (other than "on" and "off") will be possible;

c. Microphones and speakers, with amplification;

d. Stagehands to operate light and sound equipment, and to set up a simple arrangement of chairs, podium, table, etc., on an area of the stage to be determined by the Theatre;

e. Ushers to serve the audience in a nonreserved seating arrangement;

f. At Theatre's sole discretion, either (i) a stage backdrop or curtains, (ii) a bare stage, (iii) the set of the attraction currently playing the Theatre, or a combination of the same.

2. The Producer will provide and pay for:

a. A quality program approximately one (1) hour in length, of a non-commercial nature;

b. Securing, delivering, and removing any materials, such as chairs, podiums, tables, or such other furniture needed for the program (except as may have been provided for otherwise). No materials may be delivered to the Theatre before ____:____ AM, and all materials must be removed no later than ____:____, the day of the Program. All such materials must be approved by the Theatre in advance;

c. Producer will obtain and pay for all necessary performance licenses (e.g. ASCAP, B.M.I., etc.) for its Program;

d. A liaison with the Theatre's public relations office;

e. Promotional materials and information, and promotion for the Program through appropriate channels. Media and other promotional plans must be cleared with the public relations office at the Theatre. All announcements to any media, including but not limited to, press releases, programs, and invitations, will acknowledge the joint nature of this Program as follows:

—(more)—

<u>Typeface size</u>

Producer and _____ Theatre present   100%
Name of Program   100%

That is, the Producer and the Theatre shall receive equal prominence in all billing.

3.   Both parties agree to the following:

a. Admission will be without charge;

b. Seating will not be reserved, except that both Theatre and Producer may set aside a reasonable number of seats for specific guests;

c. Producer may provide additional host/ushers, at his sole expense, to aid in conducting the Program. Such personnel shall work with the approval of the Theatre;

d. The Program will begin at 12:00 noon and end between 1:00 PM and 1:15 PM, except as otherwise mutually agreed;

e. Theatre, in its sole discretion, shall exclusively display the seal and logo of the Theatre on any podium, table, and/or backdrop used in the Program;

f. There will be no charge made by either party to the other, and the parties are prohibited from charging or causing any expenses to each other or in any way financially obligating the other party except as specifically agreed to in writing. Either party has the sole right to incur its own expense.

4. The Producer shall neither sell nor distribute any information or thing of value in or around the Theatre building without prior consent of the Theatre.

5. Producer shall not assign or transfer his rights under this agreement to any other person, without prior written permission of the Theatre. Producer shall not offer any program other than the one specified in this agreement, without express written consent of the Theatre.

6. Producer promises to pay for all damages to the theatre, scenery, or other property and equipment, caused by the presentation's participants and to remove the presentation and all its equipment and props from the premises at the designated time, so as not to interfere with the next activity of the theatre. Theatre reserves the right to require a damage deposit or to cancel the presentation, whenever in its judgement, a presentation contemplated herein may pose a danger to the theatre, people in and around the theatre, scenery, or other property and equipment. This right is discretionary and will not be exercised unreasonably.

7. Should any matter or condition beyond the reasonable control of either party occur (such as, but not limited to, public emergency or calamity, strike, labor disturbance, fire, interruption of utility or transportation service, casualty, physical disability, illness, earthquake, flood, Act of God, or other disturbance, or any governmental restriction), then the presentation shall be canceled. All other existing obligations agreed upon by the parties, such as reimbursement of expenditures, continue to bind the parties. In such event, the terms of this agreement shall not be extended and Theatre shall not be obligated to provide

—(more)—

its facilities to the Guest Producer for use at a later time.

8.   The Producer shall comply with all laws, rules, regulations, and contracts of the Theatre regarding labor as may be applicable to operations contemplated under this agreement.

9.   The Producer shall indemnify, save and hold harmless the Theatre from any liability, damages, or claims resulting from: (i) the violation or infringement of any copyright, right of privacy or other statutory or common law right of any person, firm, or corporation; (ii) the defamation of any person, firm, or corporation; (iii) any and all loss and/or damage to the theatre caused by the Producer and/or by participants.

10.   Neither the Theatre nor the Producer may contract for, nor make arrangements for, radio or television broadcasting, filming, videotaping, audio recording, or any other kind of reproduction where the purpose is for commercial use or sponsorship, without the prior written consent of both the Theatre and the Producer.

11.   Producer shall comply with all rules and regulations governing the theatre and with all rules, laws, ordinances, regulations, and orders of governmental authorities. Producer shall comply with directives of the Theatre in regard to health, safety and security matters at the theatre.

12.   The references to "Theatre" and "Producer", unless otherwise specified, shall include their respective officers, Directors or Trustees, employees, agents and independent contractors.

IN WITNESS THEREOF the parties hereto have caused this Agreement to be executed by their authorized officers.

For the Theatre: For the Producer:

_____   _____

_____   _____
Title   Title

                                                  _____

                                                  _____

                                                  _____
                                                  Address

Theatre License Agreement

In consideration of the mutual promises made herein, this agreement entered into on this _____ day of _____, 19__, by and between the _____, ("Theatre"), and _____, ("Producer"), the presenter of _____ ("Attraction").

1.   Licensed Use: Theatre hereby licenses to Producer and Producer hereby licenses from Theatre the use of the theatre for performance(s), and rehearsals for the period beginning _____, 19___ and ending _____, 19___ inclusive (or as otherwise specified).

2.   Share of Receipts:

a. Of the net box office receipts, the Theatre shall receive _____ (___%), and the Producer shall receive _____ (___%).

b. The Theatre shall pay to Producer _____ dollars ($_____) for each performance in the theatre.

c. The Producer shall pay to Theatre _____ dollars ($_____) for each performance in the theatre.

d. The Producer shall pay to Theatre _____dollars ($_____) for _____.

3.   Advertising:

a.   All advertising, mutually agreed upon, not exceeding the sum of _____ _____ dollars ($_____) weekly is to be shared between the parties in the same proportion the box office receipts are shared.

b. Theatre shall pay _____ (___%) of all advertising.

c. Producer shall pay _____ (___%) of all advertising.

d. Promotional materials and information must be approved by the Theatre. All announcements to any media, including press releases, programs, posters, heralds, advertisements, and invitations, must acknowledge this engagement as follows:

	Typeface %
Attraction	100%
Producer	75%
Theatre	75%

The three identifiers indicated above may appear in any order, but must be consistent for the engagement.

4.   Services Provided by Theatre:

a. The Theatre agrees to present the Attraction and to furnish for that purpose the theatre, lighted, heated and cleaned; with ushers, ticket sellers, tickets, one (or more) stagehand(s), and regular house license.

—(more)—

b. The stage area of the theatre shall become available to the Producer for the taking in of scenery on the _____ (day) preceding the first performance, unless scheduled otherwise.

c. The auditorium and stage areas shall be available to the Producer beginning one hour before scheduled curtain time for each performance after the first, until the conclusion of each performance (including the first). Rehearsals shall be for four (4) hours, at times mutually agreed upon. Extra hours shall be paid for at the rate specified.

5.   Services Provided by Producer:

a. The Producer agrees to furnish the attraction for presentation in the theatre including, but not limited to, complete cast of characters, scenic production, all costumes, the legal permit of the author for said performance, and everything necessary to the performances not herein agreed to be furnished by the Theatre, and to give said performances in a proper and creditable manner.

b. Producer will not deliver any scenic elements or physical materials for the Attraction until the time it is scheduled to be received at the theatre. All materials belonging to the Production must be removed promptly after the final performance in the theatre.

c. Producer will designate one individual Manager who shall be responsible to Theatre as official agent of the Producer.

d. All expenses incurred by the Theatre directly or indirectly as a result of the use of the theatre building by the Producer, excepting only those expenses or costs specifically set forth in this contract as a responsibility of the Theatre, shall be paid by the Producer.

e. All personnel of the Producer shall abide by and conform to the rules of this contract, and the Producer will pay for breakage or damage to property sustained or caused by such personnel.

f. The Producer shall comply with directives of the theatre in regard to health, safety and security matters at the theatre and with all written rules and regulations relating to the building. This provision shall be enforceable by the Theatre and failure thereof shall be grounds for immediate termination of this contract.

g. All electrical equipment, scenery and property brought into the theatre by the Producer to be used in the attraction shall comply with and conform to all the Building and Fire Codes applicable to theatre. All scenery and materials shall be fireproofed prior to this engagement by the Producer according to_____ state and _____ City fire prevention standards. Upon failure of the Producer to promptly correct any such violation, the Theatre reserves the right to correct such violation at the sole expense of the Producer.

h. The Producer shall comply with all rules and regulations governing the theatre and with all rules, laws, ordinances, regulations and orders of governmental authorities, including non-discrimination requirements. The Theatre shall not be liable to the Producer for damages resulting from any diminution or deprivation of Producer's rights under this Contract on account of the exercise of any such authority as provided in this paragraph.

i. The Producer shall indemnify, save and hold harmless the Theatre from any liability, damages, or claims resulting from: (i) the violation or infringement of any copyright, right of privacy or other statutory or common law right of any person, firm, or corporation; (ii) the

—(more)—

defamation of any person, firm, or corporation; (iii) any and all loss and/or damage to the theatre caused by the Producer and/or by participants.

6. Concessions:

The Producer shall neither sell nor distribute any information or thing of value, including programs, in or around the theatre building without the prior written consent of the theatre. (Consent may be in the form of a letter.)

7. Box Office and Tickets:

a. The methods of sale and disposition of tickets shall be under the exclusive control of Theatre unless otherwise agreed in writing. The scale of tickets shall be subject to the approval of the Theater. Theatre shall have sole and exclusive control and supervision of the box office and its personnel, and all gross receipts shall, until such time as settlement is made, be under the absolute control, disposition and supervision of Theatre. All tickets, two-for-one tickets, and any other documents evidencing or affecting the right of admission to the Theatre, shall be ordered only by Theatre and the Producer covenants that it will not order, distribute and/or issue same without Theatre's prior written consent.

b. No tickets are to be sold or distributed at cut rate, two-for-one tickets, or in any other manner at less than box office price, nor shall the Producer make any arrangements of any nature whatsoever for or involving the sale of tickets without the prior written consent of the Theatre.

c. Sales commissions, including credit cards and agency, group and/or subscription sales charges shall be deducted from gross receipts, after taxes on the box office statement for each performance and shall be excluded from the computation, if any, of weekly box office receipts. Notwithstanding the foregoing, the attraction agrees to participate in the Theatre's regular Special Patron Ticket Program.

d. The free admission, if any, except to local press, shall be subject to mutual agreement.

8. Special Provisions:

_____

9. This Contract shall not be changed, modified, or varied except by a written statement signed by all parties hereto.

IN WITNESS HEREOF the parties hereto have set hands and seals the day and year first above written:

For the Theatre: For the Attraction:

_____   _____

_____   _____

_____   _____

Broadway Touring Contract

THIS AGREEMENT made and entered into this _____ day of _____, 19___ by and between _____, Manager of and Presenter in the _____ Theatre, party of the first part (sometimes referred to as the "Theatre"), and _____, jointly the party of the second part, and the producer or presenter of _____ (sometimes referred to as the "Attraction").

WITNESSETH that the party of the first part agrees to present the Attraction and to furnish for the purposes herein named said Theatre, lighted, heated, and cleaned; with ushers, ticket sellers, coupon and regular tickets, house programs and regular house license for a period beginning the _____ day of _____, 19___ and ending the _____ day of _____, 19___ inclusive (or as hereinafter specified), said engagement comprising regular evening and matinee performances.

The party of the second part, for and in consideration of One Dollar to him or them in hand paid, the receipt of which is hereby acknowledged, and for further consideration hereinafter named, agrees to furnish the Attraction for presentation by the Theatre including, but not limited to, complete scenic production, and everything necessary to the performances contemplated by this contract, not herein agreed to be furnished by the party of the first part, and to give said performances in a proper and creditable manner, with complete cast of characters and chorus, and all costumes for the same; also to furnish all perishable properties and spot, floods and any other form of lamps and electrical equipment required; also to furnish scene and property plots and the music parts for orchestra at least two weeks in advance of this engagement, provide the legal permit of the author for said performance, and pay author's fees; also to furnish and deliver to the party of the first part, at least two weeks prior to the beginning of the engagement, the necessary printed matter, properly lined and dated, photographs, press matter, cuts and any special devices that may be used by the party of the second part in sufficient quantity, for advertising said performances and receive in full consideration thereof:

1. Percentage of Receipts

a. _____ percent (____%) of the box office receipts weekly; or

b._____percent (____%)of the first_____ dollars ($_____), and _____percent (____%) of all over that amount of the box office receipts weekly.

> (1) If the box office receipts weekly, however, shall be less than the sum of _____ dollars ($_____), then and in that event the party of the second part is to receive only _____ _____ percent (____%) of the box office receipts weekly instead of any other share.

> (2) In the event, however, that the box office receipts weekly shall be less than the sum of_____dollars ($_____), then and in that event the party of the second part is to receive only _____ percent (_____%) of the box office receipts weekly instead of any other share.

If less than eight (8) performances shall be given during any week, including opening week,

—(more)—

any sums to be paid by Theatre weekly pursuant to this contract shall be reduced by one-eighth (1/8) for each performance less than eight (8) given during such week.

Party of the second part will furnish all personnel required to be employed by the party of the second part pursuant to all union rules and regulations in force at the time of the presentation of the Attraction.

The parties agree that all expenses incurred by the party of the first part directly or indirectly as a result of, or partially as a result of, the use of the theatre building by the party of the second part, excepting only those expenses or costs specifically set forth in this contract as a responsibility of the party of the first part, shall be paid by the party of the second part.

The Theatre may withhold such sums as the Theatre may determine in its absolute discretion should be withheld under the Internal Revenue Code and under other laws without liability to party of the second part as a result thereof. Notwithstanding the foregoing, the party of the second part shall withhold all taxes required to be withheld under the Internal Revenue Code and under other laws, including taxes on non-resident aliens and foreign corporations. The party of the second part shall save and hold harmless the Theatre from any and all claims and expenses relating to tax withholding requirements, including reasonable attorney's fees, that arise or are incurred as a result of the Attraction.

2. Guarantee

a. The party of the second part hereby guarantees that the share of the box office receipts to which the party of the first part shall be entitled shall not be less than the sum of _____ _____ dollars ($_____) weekly; and the party of the second part agrees that if the party of the first part's share of the box office receipts shall fall below the sum of _____ dollars ($_____) weekly, the party of the second part will pay to the party of the first part's share of the box office receipts for such week(s) and said sum of _____ dollars ($_____).

b. Notwithstanding anything to the contrary contained in this agreement, it is understood that the party of the first part shall have a first prior lien in and to any and all receipts from whatever source taken in by the party of the first part up to the amount of _____ dollars ($_____) weekly, the weekly guarantee made by the party of the second part, and that said monies shall be paid immediately upon receipt to the party of the first part.

c. The party of the second part has deposited with the party of the first part the sum of _____ dollars ($_____) to insure the faithful performance of all the terms, conditions and covenants of this agreement. Provided the party of the second part does not default in any way, the said sum shall be applied on account of the guarantee for the final week(s) of this engagement. Theatre, in its sole discretion, shall have the right at any time prior to the opening of the Attraction to demand an additional deposit from the party of the second part in an amount equal to Theatre's estimate of the cost of the expenses to be incurred by the party of the second part prior to the opening date for which Theatre may be responsible including, but not limited to, salaries of musicians and stagehands for rehearsals and preview performances.

If and when the star or featured player (or any or all of the stars or featured players) listed in this contract leave the show or are unable to perform for any reason whatsoever, the Theatre shall receive its actual out-of-pocket operating expenses plus _____ dollars ($_____) rent each week or pro rata part thereof or

—(more)—

the percentage of the weekly box office receipts as provided in this contract, whichever is greater.

3.   Stop Clause

Commencing with the week of _____, 19__, it is understood and agreed by and between the parties hereto that should the box office receipts derived from the presentation of the attraction during any _____ (___) consecutive weeks fall below the sum of _____ dollars ($_____), then and in that event either party hereto shall have the right to terminate the herein named engagement on giving the other party _____ (____) weeks notice in writing to that effect not later than after the count-up on the night of the last performance of the week during which the box office receipts shall have fallen and on the effective date of such notice the herewith named engagement and the license of the party of the second part to the use of the theatre shall terminate.

4.   Advertising

All advertising, mutually agreed upon, not exceeding the sum of _____ _____ dollars ($_____) weekly is to be shared between the parties hereto at the pro rata sharing terms herein (if used and necessary).

5.   Stagehands and Other Employees

a. Take in. Theatre agrees to allow the party of the second part a total not to exceed _____ (_____) hours, if used and/or necessary at the local weekday rate prevailing on the day of opening, to take the production into the theatre, put it up and hang it. Should it be necessary for the production to be moved into the theatre, set up and hung on any other day than the day of opening, then any additional expense shall be paid by the party of the second part. Should it be necessary for the property of the party of the second part to be moved into the theatre on a Sunday or holiday, then the expense thereof, less the amount it would have cost the party of the first part on the opening day, shall be borne by the party of the second part unless the opening day is on a Sunday or holiday, in which instance this clause does not apply.

b. Combined take in and take out. The Theatre will pay the cost of taking the production into the theatre on the day of opening, during regular union hours, and the cost to take it out immediately after the last performance up to but not exceeding the aggregate cost of _____ ($_____) dollars, if used. The party of the second part is to pay all over that amount.

c. To work. The Theatre agrees that for the regular performance hours it will provide and pay for

   (1) necessary stagehands;

   (2) not to exceed _____ (_____) stagehands, if used and necessary; such stagehands to include head carpenter, head propertyman, and their assistants, if any, and head electrician.

d. Take out. Theatre is to:

   (1) provide and pay for necessary stagehands; or

—(more)—

(2) allow the party of the second part a total of not to exceed _____
(_____) hours, if used and necessary, to take down and take out the Attraction's scenery and baggage immediately after the last performance.

Notwithstanding any weekly settlement, if any union shall subsequently require the payments by the party of the first part of any additional compensation for any employee payable under this agreement, the additional amount shall be borne by the parties hereto in the same manner as the original compensation is required to be borne by them.

If the term of the engagement commences after a dark week then the party of the second part must share pro rata on the cost of preliminary box office expenses, including first and second treasurers, box office and mail order personnel, manager, porter, watchman, light, heat and any other out-of-pocket expenses for which Theatre may be obligated by reason of union agreements, or otherwise, during such week prior to the commencement of the engagement.

Party of the second part shall comply with all laws, rules, regulations, and contracts of the Theatre regarding labor as are applicable to operations contemplated under this Contract.

The party of the second part further agrees that all personnel of the Attraction shall abide by and conform to the rules of this contract, and that the party of the second party will pay for breakage or damage to property sustained or caused by such personnel.

6. Concessions

The party of the second part shall neither sell nor distribute any information or thing of value, including programs, in or around the Theatre building without the prior written consent of the Theatre.

7. Equipment and Safety

All electrical equipment, scenery and property brought into the theatre by the party of the second part to be used in the presentation of the aforementioned production, shall comply with and conform to all the rules and regulations of the local Board of Fire Underwriters, the ordinances, statutes and laws of the _____ [state or local jurisdiction], and to the rules, regulations and directives issued by every government bureau or agency exercising jurisdiction thereover. All scenery and paraphernalia shall be fireproofed prior to this engagement by the party of the second part. The party of the first part reserves the right to correct any violation placed upon said equipment, at the sole expense of the party of the second part, upon failure of the party of the second part to comply promptly in correcting any such violation.

The party of the second part shall comply with directives of the theatre in regard to health, safety and security matters at the Theatre and with all written rules and regulations relating to the building. This provision shall be enforceable by the party of the first part and failure hereof shall be grounds for immediate termination of this contract.

8. Box Office and Tickets

The Theatre agrees to furnish treasurer and assistant treasurer. In case it should be necessary to engage a second assistant treasurer in the box office during this engagement, the salary of the second assistant treasurer shall be shared by both parties in the same percentage as they share in the box office receipts. It is agreed that any expense for box

—(more)—

office help over and above the aforementioned will be paid for by the party of the second part. Both parties hereto also agree to share at the pro rata sharing terms herein on the cost of the clerks called in to take care of the mail orders and the cost of postage, envelopes, and other expenses in connection with processing mail orders.

The box office receipts of each performance shall be ascertained by the statement of the sale at the box office verified by the count of the tickets taken at the doors, and settlement may be made at the end of each week, or at such other times as shall be mutually agreed upon by the parties hereto.

The methods of sale and disposition of tickets shall be under the exclusive control of Theatre unless otherwise agreed in writing. The scale of tickets shall be subject to the approval of the Theater. Theatre shall have sole and exclusive control and supervision of the box office and its personnel, and all gross receipts shall, until such time as settlement is made, be under the absolute control, disposition and supervision of Theatre. All tickets, two-for-one tickets, and any other documents evidencing or affecting the right of admission to the Theatre, shall be ordered only by Theatre and the party of the second party covenants that it will not order, distribute and/or issue same without Theatre's prior written consent. No tickets are to sold or distributed at cut rate, two-for-one tickets, or in any other manner at less than box office price, nor shall the party of the second part make any arrangements of any nature whatsoever for or involving the sale of tickets without the prior written consent of the Theatre. Sales commissions, including credit cards and agency, group and/or subscription sales charges shall be deducted from gross receipts, after taxes on the box office statement for each performance and shall be excluded from the computation, if any, of weekly box office receipts.

Notwithstanding the foregoing, the Attraction agrees to participate in the Theatre's regular Special Patron Ticket program.

It is understood and agreed by and between the parties hereto, the box office receipts referred to herein shall be monies paid by the actual patrons of the theatre and neither party hereto shall have the right to add to or subtract from these receipts for the purpose of changing the percentage or for any purpose whatsoever, except that an amount equivalent to the local sales tax, sales commissions (including credit cards), and agency, group and/or subscription sales charges shall be deducted from box office receipts on the box office statement for each performance and shall be excluded for the computation, if any, of weekly box office receipts.

The free admission, if any, except to local press, shall be subject to mutual agreement.

9. Special Provisions

_____
_____
_____
_____

10. Miscellaneous

The party of the second part shall comply with all rules and regulations governing the theatre and with all rules, laws, ordinances, regulations and orders of governmental authorities, including non-discrimination requirements. The Theatre shall not be liable to the party of the second part for damages resulting from any diminution or deprivation of party of the second part's rights under this Contract on account of the exercise of any such authority as provided in this paragraph.

—(more)—

During the time this Attraction is playing at the Theatre, the party of the second part will fully insure itself, its officers, directors, employees, agents, and the company, at its own expense, as follows: Worker's Compensation and Employer's Liability (including disability benefits), comprehensive general liability (personal injury, including bodily injury, $_____ per occurrence; and property damage, $_____ per occurrence); and theft and fire insurance (with the applicable standard extended coverage clause) for all properties brought into the theatre including the property of third persons under the control of the party of the second part. The fire insurance policy shall include a waiver of subrogation against the party of the first part and any entity or person affiliated with the party of the first part. All liability policies shall name the party of the first part as an insured. Upon request certificates of insurance evidencing such coverage shall be furnished to the party of the first part at least twenty-one (21) days prior to party of the second part's first use of the Theatre and the party of the second part shall furnish actual policies on demand. All policies shall be endorsed to provide a thirty (30) day notice of cancellation or material change to the party of the first part. No rehearsals or presentations shall be conducted or presented until the required insurance coverage is in effect.

The party of the second part further agrees that, except at the Theatre hereinabove named, the party of the second part will not allow the attraction to appear, play or perform, or to be advertised to appear, play or perform, or to render any professional service, or be advertised in any way as an attraction at any theatre, cabaret or other place of amusement, restaurant, or other place patronized by the public, including clubs or benefits, whether a charge is made by such places or not, nor to render any service in connection with any broadcasting or by cable or by any mechanical, electrical, or electronic means now known or hereafter coming into existence, prior to this engagement in the city [or community] named above, during the run at said Theatre and for a period of eight (8) weeks succeeding the termination of the engagement at the said theatre named in this contract, without the prior written consent of the party of the first part. In case the party of the second part violates this condition the party of the second part hereby agrees to pay said party of the first part as liquidated, stipulated, and agreed damages, and in no way as a penalty, the sum of _____ ($_____) per week as partial damages, and the party of the second part consents that in the event of his breach of this clause, that the party of the first part may obtain an injunction from any court of competent jurisdiction, restraining the advertising of or the appearance of the Attraction, at any other theatre for the term, and that the party of the second part will interpose no defense thereto. And it is further agreed, that in case the said party of the first part has any money in his hand belonging to the party of the second part, the amount of said agreed damages may be retained and applied to the payment thereof.

The party of the second part, and each of them, shall be jointly and severally liable to Theatre for any damages sustained by Theatre by reason of failure of the party of the second part to perform its obligations under this contract.

Should any matter or condition beyond the reasonable control of either party ("force majeure"), such as, but not limited to, war, public emergency or calamity, strike, labor disturbance, fire, interruption of transportation service, casualty, physical disturbance, or any governmental restriction, prevent performance by a party to this contract, then the following provisions shall pertain and the parties otherwise shall respectively be relieved of their obligations under this contract:

(a) If such force majeure shall prevent performance by party of the second part but not prevent performance by party of the first part, party of the second part shall continue to be obligated to make all payments required of party of the second part under this contract as if such force majeure shall not have occurred and to perform all of its other obligations arising

—(more)—

under this contract to the extent reasonably possible in the face of such force majeure.

(b) If such force majeure shall otherwise prevent performance by a party or parties: (i) party of the second part shall continue to be obligated to perform all of its payment obligations arising under this contract but performance of all of its other obligations arising under this contract shall be suspended or excused to the extent commensurate with such force majeure; and (ii) Theatre's obligations arising under this contract shall be suspended or excused to the extent commensurate with such force majeure.

(c) In the event of such force majeure, the term of this contract shall not be extended and Theatre shall not be obligated to furnish the theatre or any part of the building to party of the second part for use during any other period in substitution for the period, if any, when performance is prevented by such force majeure.

In the event of the herein-named Theatre being closed, because of further rehearsals of the attraction or on account of sickness or inability of the principal performer, or for any other cause whatsoever, excepting only as recited in the preceding paragraph then the party of the second part shall pay reasonable rent for the said theatre for the time closed, and in addition thereto all other expenses of every name or nature incurred by the party of the first part for the purpose of the party of the second part, or for their joint interest in the attraction to be played hereunder.

Any notice that the parties may desire or may be required under this contract shall be deemed sufficiently given if in writing and personally delivered or sent by registered or certified mail, return receipt requested, postage prepaid, addressed to the addressee at the mailing address as specified for the parties in this contract, or such other address as the parties may designate by written notice. The time of the delivery of such notice shall be deemed to be the time when the same is so mailed or personally delivered.

If any provision of this contract or its application to any person or in any circumstances shall be invalid or unenforceable, the other provisions of this contract shall not be effected by such invalidity or unenforceability.

Any provision of this contract to the contrary notwithstanding, it is the intention of the parties that legal title in the space and facilities made available to the party of the second part for its use shall remain vested in the Theatre building and that no interest of the party of the second part in real property shall be created by this Contract; that such contract rights as are given to the party of the second part by this Contract shall not be construed to imply any authority, privilege, or right to operate or engage in any business or activity other than as provided by this Contract, and that none of the space of facilities permitted to the party of the second part for its use is leased to the party of the second part.

The terms "party of the first part" and "party of the second part", unless otherwise specified shall include their respective officers, directors or trustees, employees, agents and independent contractors. The term "patrons" shall include all persons who are not employees of the parties and who are present in the Theatre partially or wholly for the purpose of purchasing tickets for the Attraction and/or attending the Attraction, and/or of performing services related to the Attraction, and/or for any other reason related to or arising from the Attraction.

This Contract shall not be changed, modified, or varied except by a written instrument signed by all parties hereto.

—(more)—

IN WITNESS HEREOF the parties hereto have set hands and seals the day and year first above written:

For the Theatre: For the Attraction:

_____   _____

_____   _____

_____   _____

Form 2-11

Producer's Booking Contract

Agreement made this _____ day of _____, 19__, by and between _____ (hereinafter referred to as "Producer"), and _____ (hereinafter referred to as "Theatre").

The parties agree to the following:

1. Producer agrees to furnish _____ (hereinafter called "Attraction") upon the terms and conditions set forth.

2. The Attraction shall perform at the Theatre at the dates and times indicated on the schedule attached to this agreement, at the box office prices indicated on the schedule attached to this agreement.

3. It is agreed that as full compensation for providing the Attraction as set forth, Theatre will pay to Producer the sum of $_____ per week plus _____% over $_____ gross receipts each week. Overages, if any, are payable immediately following the last performance of each week. _____ dollars ($_____) shall be paid to Producer upon execution of this agreement by Theatre, with the balance of the guarantee payable _____ (number of days) before the first performance.

4. Theatre warrants and represents that it has or will have a valid lease or license for the place of performance covering the date(s) of this engagement, proof of which will be given to Producer upon request.

5. Gross Receipts:

a. If Producer's payment is based, in whole or in part, upon a percentage of the gross box office receipts, it is agreed the computation of gross receipts shall exclude a) government admission taxes, b) credit card commissions, and c) ticket agency, ticket broker, or group sales agency commissions, but only where such agencies or brokers are not affiliated with Theatre.

b. If Theatre does not use a computer system, Theatre agrees to have any and all preprinted admission tickets for this engagement printed by a recognized, bonded ticket printing company and Theatre shall furnish Producer with a certified copy of the ticket manifest. Such manifest will be supplied to Producer before any tickets are sold for this engagement.

c. Unless otherwise agreed to in writing by Producer, the house will be sold on a reserved-seat basis, with all tickets numbered by seat according to the house seating chart. A copy of said house seating chart is attached to this agreement. No seats are to be on the stage during a performance.

d. Theatre shall not give more than _____ (_____) complimentary tickets for each performance for press, and Theatre shall supply Producer with an exact list of those to whom complimentary tickets are given.

e. Under no circumstances are any tickets to be discounted in any manner whatsoever without the express written consent of Producer.

—(more)—

f. If, for any reason, Producer questions the means or methods used by Theatre in preparing the box office statement in connection with this engagement, then Producer shall have the right, should it so desire, to base any earned percentages due under the terms of the contract upon the number of ticket stubs collected by the ticket takers and those attendees estimated by Producer as admitted free.

g. The Producer shall have the right to be present in the box office at any time tickets are sold to the Attraction. The producer shall be given full access to observe all box office sales and shall otherwise be permitted reasonably to be satisfied as to the gross receipts at each performance hereof including the right to observe ticket racks (if any), all box office and other records with respect to ticket sales including any unsold tickets and stubs of tickets sold. While in the box office, Producer is not authorized to touch anything.

h. Final payment shall be accompanied by an accurate box office statement prepared for each performance of this engagement and signed by the box office treasurer and the Theatre manager. If the box office is computer operated, one copy of the instruction manual shall be provided to the Producer.

6. In general, the Theatre agrees to furnish at its sole cost and expense:

a. The Theatre on the date(s) and at the time(s) indicated on the attached schedule, properly heated or air conditioned, lighted, clean and in good order, with clean, comfortable dressing rooms near the stage for exclusive use by the Attraction, and all licenses and fees therefor;

b. Ushers, ticket takers, ticket sellers, and any other box office employees required for advance and current sales, truck loaders and unloaders, stagehands, electricians, wardrobe attendants, maintenance personnel, and all other personnel to operate the Theatre during the engagement;

c. Tickets, posters, window cards, mailing and distribution of circulars, newspaper advertising in the principal newspapers in the area, and publicity and promotion services of every type required;

d. All lights, microphones, props, equipment, facilities, and other material, unless otherwise agreed to be provided by Producer.

e. Any and all charges for any musical contractor or any additional musicians as may be required by the local musicians union under whose jurisdiction this engagement is played.

f. Theatre and Producer understand that the Attraction is "yellow card" and that the Theatre is responsible to provide and pay for all personnel required by the yellow card and not supplied by the Producer. Additionally, all personnel furnished by Theatre shall be members in good standing of the applicable unions or guilds having jurisdiction.

g. In the event that the local union requests any additional sound men during the performance, Theatre agrees to employ and pay for such additional sound men.

7. Specifically, the Theatre shall furnish and provide the following at its sole cost and expense:

a. Four (4) Super Trouper Follow Spotlights, two at rear of house and two outside proscenium at sides of stage and elevated to a height to be designated by Producer with a normal complement of gelatins and four qualified and experienced operators.

—(more)—

b. A minimum of ten (10) qualified and experienced stagehands to aid in setting up and breaking down scenery and ten (10) qualified stagehands for the setting up and taking down of the stage lighting equipment to be furnished by Theatre.

c. A stage forty-eight feet (48') wide and thirty-two feet (32') deep for the exclusive use by the Producer. Theatre agrees that this stage area will be kept free of people and equipment during the time that it is assigned to the Producer. In the event that it is necessary for the Theatre to have other artists, their employees and equipment on this stage area during the time assigned to the Producer, Theatre agrees that their presence will be concealed from the audience by means of curtains, drops or screens.

d. Adequate electrical service and electrical facilities to be installed by licensed electricians and professional personnel in accordance with the standards of the community for the installation and operation in a safe manner for electrical appliances, facilities and wiring.

e. All necessary permits, licenses and authorizations from any and all government agencies, bureaus, departments, federal, state or local.

f. Two (2) teamsters or stagehands as required by local union regulations for loading and unloading equipment and access to the place of performance for the purpose of loading and unloading said equipment at time to be advised by Producer.

g. A suitable, adequate and usable communication system (such as intercom or walkie-talkie) for use in communicating between personnel located on the stage, the lighting controller and sound booth.

h. A separate communication system for the exclusive use of the Lighting Director to cue the follow-spots and the dimmer board shall also be provided. This system shall connect the lighting designer's master station headset for (a) a headset for the dimmer board operators, (b) a head set for each of the lighting tower operators, (c) a headset for each of the six or more front of house follow spot operators. At least the board operators and tower spot operator's headsets should have rubber muffs to isolate outside noise from the show from interfering with their hearing cues.

i. One (1) qualified and experienced sound man, plus one (1) additional assistant to aid in setting up, operating and breaking down Producer's sound equipment.

j. Electrical outlets capable of handling 60 amps no further than twenty (20) feet from the stage.

k. Fourteen (14) chairs and music stands with lights for the musicians.

l. Within twenty (20) feet of the stage, 3-wire single phase 220 volts and 200 amps per phase. A 30 amp outlet for sound on each side of the stage front.

m. A grand piano tuned to 440 pitch and a _____ (brand or style) electric organ with two (2) speakers.

n. Stage lighting to be furnished by Producer, at $_____ per week payable by Theatre prior to the last performance of each week.

o. Fourteen (14) musicians as per instrumentation to be furnished by Producer.

—(more)—

8.   Producer shall furnish sound equipment and Theatre shall pay Producer in addition to all other compensation the sum of $_____ per performance or $_____ weekly, at Theatre's option, as partial reimbursement of Producer's cost in furnishing said sound equipment. The aforesaid compensation shall be paid to Producer prior to the last performance of each week of the engagement. Producer's sound engineer may, at his sole discretion, use entire house sound system or portions thereof, as he deems necessary. Complete control of sound facilities and its operation during the performance shall remain in the hands of the sound engineer furnished by the Producer.

In the event any union restrictions prevent the sound man and assistant from loading and unloading the equipment called for under this agreement, Producer and Theatre agree they will abide by any union regulations that govern this matter, and Theatre assumes all costs in connection therewith.

9.   Theatre shall not allow the audience to enter the place of performance until such time as technical set up has been completed. Producer will do his utmost to have the technical set up completed at least one (1) hour prior to scheduled performance time.

10. Dressing Rooms: Theatre shall provide comfortable and private dressing rooms to accommodate thirty (30) performers as follows: two (2) dressing rooms for the four (4) principals, two (2) dressing rooms for the chorus (14 people), and one (1) dressing room for the orchestra (approximately 12 people). These rooms shall be clean, dry, well lit, heated or air conditioned, shall each contain make-up mirrors and sinks with hot and cold running water, and sufficient chairs for the number of people in each dressing room, and shall be within easy access to well heated, clean, private lavatories which are supplied with soap, toilet tissue and towels. These lavatories shall be closed to the general public. Theatre shall be solely responsible for the security of the dressing area and shall keep all unauthorized persons from entering the area.

11. Advertising and Promotion:

a. Producer agrees to supply the usual quantity of printing and advertising material available for the promotion of the Attraction.

b. Theatre agrees to adhere to the following billing requirements in all manner and forms of advertising in connection with the engagement including, but not limited to tickets, paid newspaper advertising, publicity releases, programs, fliers, posters, signs, billboard and marquees. No other name or names shall be billed or used in connection with the engagement without the express written consent of Producer. It is specifically understood that the same style of boldness, thickness and color of type will be used throughout and in the relative sizes as specified below:

50%	THEATRE NAME Presents
100%	TITLE
75%	Music By COMPOSER'S NAME

—(more)—

c. Theatre agrees to submit to Producer three (3) copies of all printed advertisements in connection with this engagement.

12. Attraction:

a. Producer shall have the sole and exclusive control over the Attraction, presentation and performance of the engagement hereunder.

b. It is specifically agreed that Producer shall have sole and absolute authority in mixing and controlling all sound equipment during the performance and rehearsal of this engagement.

c. Producer shall give all light cues and shall have final approval on staging.

d. In the event there are any local union charges in connection with any of the personnel or services provided by Theatre, Theatre agrees to assume all costs in connection therewith.

e. Producer reserves the sole, exclusive, and irrevocable right to the sale of all program books, posters, recordings, articles of clothing or jewelry, or other souvenirs during this engagement. The distribution and/or sale of any program book, souvenir or give-away other than Producer's program book must be approved in advance by Producer.

13. Rehearsal: Theatre agrees to make available at Theatre's sole cost and expense the place of engagement (theatre, auditorium, and all stage areas) for rehearsal during the first day of the engagement in each city. Rehearsal time will be from noon through 6:00 p.m. the day of the engagement, which will be at Theatre's sole cost and expense. Theatre further agrees to furnish for this rehearsal at its sole cost and expense all personnel required for full and complete rehearsal including, but not limited to, musicians, house electricians, spot light operators, and stage hands whether or not required by local union agreements.

14. Cancellations:

a. Producer reserves the right to cancel this engagement not later than forty-five (45) days prior to play date by notice in writing to Theatre, without any cost, obligation, or penalty to Producer. It is further understood and agreed that failure by Theatre to fulfill any of the above or below mentioned requirements or any material breach of this agreement may result in the cancellation of said engagement at anytime without penalty whatsoever to Producer.

b. In the event Theatre refuses or neglects to provide any of the items herein stated, or fails or refuses to make any of the payments as provided herein or to proceed with the engagement, Producer shall have no obligation to perform this contract, and shall retain any amounts theretofore paid to Producer or in his behalf by Theatre, and Theatre shall remain liable to Producer for the contract price herein set forth.

c. The performing personnel shall not be required to appear and perform before any audience that is segregated on the basis of race, color, religion, sex, or national origin, or where physical violence or injury is likely to occur. If any of the foregoing conditions exist and the performing personnel do not appear or perform as a result, the same shall not constitute a breach of this agreement by Producer.

d. In the event of sickness or of accident to performer(s) in the Attraction, or if a

—(more)—

performance is prevented, rendered impossible or infeasible, by any act or regulation of any public authority or bureau, tumult, strike, epidemic, interruption in or delay of transportation, war condition or emergencies, or any cause beyond the control of Producer, it is understood and agreed that there shall be no claims for damages by either party to this contract, and Producer's obligation to such performance shall be deemed waived. In the event of such non-performance for any of the reasons stated in this paragraph, the monies (if any) advanced to Producer hereunder, shall be returned on a pro rata basis, based upon the number of performances given. Inclement weather rendering performance impossible or infeasible shall not be deemed an emergency and payment of the agreed upon price shall be made; provided, however, that Producer is ready, willing, and able to perform pursuant to the terms hereof.

15. No portion of performance contracted hereunder may be photographed, recorded, filmed, taped or recorded in any form for the purpose of reproducing such performances, and Theatre agrees that it will not authorize or permit any such recording to be made. Attraction's name or likeness shall not be used as an endorsement of any product or service nor in connection with any commercial tie-in without Producer's prior written consent.

16. In the case of any conflict of terms, the terms contained in this contract shall prevail over any other contract or rider attached hereto. All terms of this contract are specifically accepted by Theatre unless they are waived and such waiver shall be effective only if initialed by both Producer and Theatre.

17. All notices required hereunder shall be given in writing by registered or certified mail. If to Producer, notices shall be addressed to _____; if to theatre, notices shall be addressed to _____.

18. This contract cannot be assigned or transferred without the written consent of Producer. It contains the complete understanding of the parties hereto, and may not be amended, supplemented, varied or discharged, except by an instrument in writing signed by both parties. The validity, construction and effect of this contract shall be governed by the laws of the State of New York, regardless of place of performance. This contract is not binding upon the parties until executed and delivered by Producer to Theatre. The terms "Producer," "Attraction," and "Theatre" as used herein shall include and apply to the singular and the plural and to all genders, and to all representatives, employees, and agents of each party.

19. Except for such circumstances as either party may require equitable relief to prevent irresponsible harm, any claim or a breach hereunder will be decided by a single arbitrator in New York City under the rules of the American Arbitration Association then operating under the rules of the State of New York and shall be enforceable and binding on both parties to this contract. In the event of arbitration the prevailing party shall be entitled to recover any and all reasonable attorney's fees and other costs incurred in the enforcement of the terms of this contract or the breach thereof.

20. It is agreed that Producer signs this contract as an independent contractor, and shall have the exclusive control over the methods employed in fulfilling his obligations hereunder, in all respects and in all detail. This contract shall not, in any way, be construed so as to create a partnership, or any other kind of joint undertaking or venture between the parties hereto.

For the Theatre:

—(more)—

Name:_____

Title:_____

Address:_____

_____

_____

For the Producer:

Name:_____

Title:_____

Address:_____

_____

_____

Form 2-12

Memorandum

To: Theatre manager

Subject: Use of rehearsal room

When current attractions are not using the rehearsal room, the room may be rented to other groups according to the following schedule:

By the hour: _____ (_____) hour minimum at $_____ per hour (including breaks).

By the day: 10:00 AM to midnight at $_____ per day.

By the week: Monday - Saturday, 10:00 to Midnight, $_____.

In addition, if the theatre is otherwise closed during the day or days the rehearsal room is used, the renter must pay for a stage doorman for those hours needed. Any costs for stagehands or other expenses will be charged to renter. Normal housekeeping is included in fees.

Form 2–13

Special Events Reservation

Date_____ Time_____

Organization_____

Contact_____ Telephone_____

Address_____

_____

Nature of Event_____

_____

Food service_____

Deliver time for food and equipment_____

Room requested_____

Performance attended_____

Type of event_____

Room rental fee_____

Equipment needed_____

_____

Equipment rental fee_____

Theatre tour_____ Speech_____

Show tickets needed (contact group sales)_____

Deposit due by_____ Amount_____

Balance due by_____ Amount_____

Notes:

Theatre Contact_____

Form 2–14

Chapter 3
Front of House

"The play's the thing!" a manager once said. But he used that as an excuse to ignore trash on the floor, no paper in the rest rooms, and homemade cookies as concession food. He also wondered why his shows never sold many tickets.

Second only to the box office, the front of house operation has the most direct impact on the audience, for good or bad. But it needs to be good. Ushers, ticket takers, concessionaires, and other front of house personnel, whether volunteer or paid, are easy to find and retain if they feel useful and appreciated. The best way to promote that goodwill is to be organized, have specific duties for staff to perform, and be sure each employee knows what is expected of him or her, when to do it, and what performances to work. Forms are provided in this chapter to help the house manager organize the front of house.

Many small theatres have not yet learned what the pros know very well: there is a lot of money to be made from a well run concession operation. Nevertheless, many operators have so little control on the operation that they *sell* less than the staff and cast eat. Locking up the food and drinks will help, but only good accounting procedures will help the concessionaire know where his product is going, and what items are making money and which are not. A variety of forms are provided, helping the small time—as well as the big time operator—keep track of the money.

Compare the agreement made in a theatre that operated their concessions in-house, with a contract used to hire a professional, independent company to run concessions. When done in-house, many of the protections needed by the theatre from the private company are not necessary, and the entire fee structure is different.

Why would a facility operator want to hire an outside company? Several reasons, with the main reason being to let the "professionals" do what they do best. Full time, independent concessionaires should have the experience and knowledge to do the job right. Their presence can save the theatre operator an enormous headache, and remove a time consuming activity from his own work load. Another reason to hire an outsider is to eliminate special insurance the theatre would otherwise need.

Alternatively, by keeping the activity in-house, the management can keep tight control over the operation, exercise more supervision over the staff, and, hopefully, make more money. Of course, many theatre operations are just too small to be of interest to the professional companies.

FRONT OF HOUSE SCHEDULES

The two front of house schedules, Forms 3-1 and 3-2 are self explanatory. Besides the obvious difference in staff size, in larger houses the division of labor is more pronounced. In the larger house there is a regular box office staff, a regular concession staff, a group of ushers and ticket takers, and so on. Each department has its own leader/supervisor, responsible for his or her own staff.

The large theatre may need more than a dozen ushers each performance. Form 3-2 is set up for an entire week, eight performances, with a particular work assignment for every individual. Ticket takers and concession workers are scheduled separately. Certain ushers, here called "directors," are those ushers on each seating level who hand out programs and direct patrons to the proper aisle, where other ushers will show them to their reserved seats.

For the largest houses such detail may not be prepared. Instead lists may be used, assigning individuals to certain floors or sections, with specific assignments made by a leader, or floor director, at that location.

The small theatre form assumes the house manager is responsible for scheduling all front of house jobs. That includes one ticket seller in the box office at show time, one ticket taker, one usher, and one concessionaire. The full staff is needed during the half-hour interval between the time the doors open to patrons and the curtain actually going up; however, not all the staff need stay for the duration of the show.

The ticket seller should stay on duty for about one half hour after the show begins. There are often latecomers buying tickets or picking up reservations. The ticket seller also needs to prepare a box office statement as soon as practical. Usually, the seller is finished with everything about an hour after the show starts.

The ticket taker is needed for the entire performance. While it is not likely that there will be late-comers arriving more than an hour after the scheduled curtain time, there must be a staff member on duty at all times in the theatre lobby. Throughout the course of a performance, there are often people entering the lobby, parents arriving early to pick up their kids, people walking down the street looking for directions to someplace else or just a rest room. A ticket taker is there for general security. During a performance, a lobby is usually deserted and quiet. Uninvited guests could easily enter the theatre and cause all kinds of problems. One person in the lobby is a great deterrence to strangers.

Not all ushers need stay throughout the performance, but there must be at least one usher inside the theatre at all times when an audience is present. In a multi-level theatre, there must be at least one usher on duty for each seating level, e.g. orchestra, balcony, etc. If a level has more than two or three hundred seats, two ushers may be advisable. Remind ushers they are there to help patrons, and not to be absorbed in the show, not to sleep, not to be seated in a far corner where they cannot be of help, and not to be sitting in the middle of a row where they have to climb over patrons to get in and out.

Before each performance begins, a small theatre may need only one concession sales person. But during intermission, even a small theatre may benefit from two or even three sellers. This is where you put your extra ushers or ticket sellers to productive use.

For specific duties of the staff, see the schedule and procedures in Form 3-3. This schedule generally applies to large and small theatres alike.

Front of House Staff

Attraction_____ w/e_____

Day_____   Ticket seller   _____

Time_____   Ticket taker   _____

Date_____   Usher   _____

Concessionaire   _____

Day_____   Ticket seller   _____

Time_____   Ticket taker   _____

Date_____   Usher   _____

Concessionaire   _____

Day_____   Ticket seller   _____

Time_____   Ticket taker   _____

Date_____   Usher   _____

Concessionaire   _____

Day_____   Ticket seller   _____

Time_____   Ticket taker   _____

Date_____   Usher   _____

Concessionaire   _____

Form 3–1

The Well-Run Theatre

Daily Schedule for Week of _____

ORCHESTRA

STATION	MONDAY	TUESDAY	WEDNESDAY	THURSDAY	FRIDAY	SATURDAY MATINEE	SATURDAY EVENING	SUNDAY MATINEE
LEFT AISLE								
LEFT CENTER AISLE								
RIGHT CENTER AISLE								
RIGHT AISLE								

1ST BALCONY

STATION	MONDAY	TUESDAY	WEDNESDAY	THURSDAY	FRIDAY	SATURDAY MATINEE	SATURDAY EVENING	SUNDAY MATINEE
LEFT AISLE								
LEFT AISLE								
RIGHT AISLE								
RIGHT AISLE								
DIRECTOR								

2ND BALC.

STATION	MONDAY	TUESDAY	WEDNESDAY	THURSDAY	FRIDAY	SATURDAY MATINEE	SATURDAY EVENING	SUNDAY MATINEE
LEFT AISLE								
RIGHT AISLE								
DIRECTOR								

Form 3–2

Memorandum

To: Ushers
Subject: Standard procedures

All ushers are to observe the following schedule. All times are shown for a 7:30 PM curtain.

6:30 Report to work.
      In order to open the doors on time, every usher must be on time. If you are going to be late, call the house manager in advance. As you come in, report to the Head Usher so that he/she will know you are here. If programs need stuffing, begin immediately.

6:50 Check with Head Usher for assigned position, and get a flashlight.
      At this time the Head Usher may have some specific instructions and announcements for the entire group. Everyone is to be present for this meeting.

6:55 Go to your assigned place. Take the programs for your aisle with you. Check all exit doors to be sure they are not blocked inside or out, and can open easily.

7:00 Auditorium doors open, and patrons are admitted into the house. Ushers must be at their assigned position, and should not group together or socialize. If seats are reserved, help patrons find their specific seats. Precede patrons down the aisle to their row, do not just point. Offer assistance to those patrons who have trouble with stairs. Be ladies and gentlemen.

7:30 Curtain up.

7:50 Those ushers who will remain on duty may have a ten minute break.

8:00 As ushers return from their breaks, those ushers not working the entire performance may leave. Bring all but a dozen or so unused programs back to the office. Ticket takers should check with the box office to get information on ticket orders that have not yet been picked up.

When patrons enter during the performance, be quick to turn on your flashlight and assist them in finding their seats. When a patron rises to exit during the performance, turn on your flashlight and illuminate the aisle and stairs. Be careful not to shine your light in any patron's eyes or towards the stage.

There must be an usher in the seating area at all times. If there is more than one usher on a seating level, then one may stay inside the house, while the other remains in the lobby.

Intermission: Ushers on duty should open the auditorium doors, and may move back and forth between the inner lobby and the auditorium, generally being observant and helpful. Patrons will have questions about rest rooms, refreshments, smoking, and so on.

—(more)—

When chimes sound indicating the end of the intermission is near, the ushers should position themselves at the auditorium doors, and politely inform patrons that they may not smoke nor bring drinks into the auditorium. When most of the patrons are in the house, or when the house lights go down for the next act—whichever occurs first—close the doors to the house.

Final Curtain: After the last curtain call, when the house lights come on, open all the doors. Wait in position until all patrons have left your area. After the house is empty, do the following: a) look carefully for lost or forgotten things, b) check all exit doors, making sure no one is standing right outside, and close and be certain all doors are locked, c) leave all lost and found at the office, d) return flashlight and extra programs to the office.

GENERAL RULES

1. Patrons are never allowed to stand or sit in any aisles or on stairs, or otherwise block passageways. This is dangerous to other patrons, and is a violation of fire laws.

2. Report accidents or anything out of the ordinary to the Head Usher.

3. Try to be as quiet as possible and be careful not to do anything that would disturb patrons. Talk as little as possible. If you must talk, speak softly. Try to talk to patrons in the lobby, not inside the house.

4. Handle your flashlight with care. If it needs repair or new batteries, give it to the Head Usher.

5. If a patron has a ticket that was not torn by the ticket taker, tear it properly, then give your portion to the house manager promptly.

6. Doctors or others who are expecting calls may leave their seat locations with the Head Usher. Beepers should be discouraged.

7. The taking of photographs, videotaping, or tape recording the performance is strictly forbidden. Patrons should be immediately advised of this. If they continue recording, advise the Head Usher or manager immediately.

8. Always be aware of patrons with limited mobility, particularly those who need wheelchairs, walkers, or crutches to move. Note that wheelchairs may be placed only in certain aisle locations, and may never block an aisle in another location. Assistance may be provided in helping an individual move from a wheelchair to a theatre seat. Empty wheelchairs should generally be moved to a safe location at the back of the house. Crutches may not be left in an aisle but may be placed under the feet of the patron while seated. At all times be aware of tripping hazards!

If you are not staying the entire performance, be sure the usher who is staying knows the locations of all patrons with wheelchairs or crutches, or those who need other special assistance.

—(more)—

At intermission, ask the patron if he or she desires to get out, and provide assistance where appropriate. After the performance, be certain to return the wheelchair to the patron, and provide additional assistance as needed.

9. Proper dress: Everyone should wear comfortable clothes and shoes, and must be neat, clean, and presentable at all times. Hair must be clean and combed. Wear no jewelry or other ornamentation that makes noise.

Women: White blouse with long sleeves and a collar, dark skirt (or pants), hose, dark shoes.

Men: Dark jacket and pants, white shirt, conservative tie, polished black shoes.

Form 3–3

Memorandum

To: Ushers
Subject: Seating late arriving patrons

For the convenience of other patrons, and to reduce the adverse impact of latecomers on the performance, one of the following plans on seating latecomers will be in effect. Before each performance, be certain you know which plan is to be used.

Continuous Seating: All latecomers are seated continuously throughout the performance. This is most common for nonmusical plays.

Seating Between Numbers: This is common for musical comedies. Late patrons are told by lobby ushers that they are permitted to enter the auditorium while the performance is in progress, but if they enter during a musical number, they must stand at the back of the house until that piece has ended. They may be seated during the applause.

Inside Hold: Similar to seating between numbers, but for ballet and opera, seating is only during a scene break or intermissions.

Outside Hold: Latecomers have their tickets torn, but are told by the ticket takers that they are admitted to the inside lobbies, but will be held outside the auditorium. This is usually done for classical concerts, some ballet, and opera. For this procedure, the ushers, at least one for each set of lobby doors, come out of the house when the show begins to stand in front of the doors until the hold is over. One usher remains inside the house, and notifies the outside usher when the seating may begin. All patrons may then enter and be seated. Ushers should check to see if another outside hold will go into effect for other latecomers. At no time during an outside hold is any usher allowed to enter or exit through those doors. When there are no more holds, ushers may return to their assigned places inside the house.

This is a very severe policy when used by the theatre management, and is not applied
—(more)—

without thought. Patrons who have paid for their tickets are always very unhappy when they are forced to miss part of the performance, sometimes for reasons beyond their control. Patrons with substantial complaints should be directed to see the Head Usher or manager. Usually, when patrons buy their tickets, they are given a small note notifying them that latecomers "will be seated at the discretion of the management."

Form 3–4

PATRON'S LOST TICKETS

When a patron loses his tickets, it can be a real headache for the box office, the theatre manager, the house manager, and the ushers.

If the patron purchased tickets by mail order or by telephone, the box office has a reliable record of exactly which seats were given to the patron. It takes only a quick check to learn the seat numbers and fill out a short form. The customer will be on his way to being seated and enjoying the show in peace and quiet, grateful for the smooth operation of the theatre management.

Unfortunately, things often do not go that smoothly. Often, the customer purchased his tickets in advance at the box office, and left no record of the seats obtained. In that case, the manager, head usher, or box office treasurer (whoever is handling such problems) must try to determine about where the seats are located. You can usually determine what seating level is involved by asking about the price paid for the tickets. If the show is not selling very well, then the patron can merely be seated towards the rear of the correct section, and probably there will be no problems.

However, if the show is close to being sold out, then you may have to get specific, unsold locations from the box office. So long as the seats are not going to be sold anyway, this is a safe procedure because you know the replacements seats will remain vacant.

When the show is sold out, there is not much you can safely do. You must not seat the people in empty seats just before the curtain goes up. You can explain to them that they may be seated, but that if customers arrive late with tickets for those seats, they will have to move. You could try that, once maybe, if you have vacant aisle seats, but it is not advised. With aisle seats, they may be willing to move once, but probably not twice, before they make camp and refuse to budge. Never place people in seats in the middle of a row. Once the curtain goes up, if they don't want to leave, you can't get them out without disturbing the performance and other patrons.

If people do not know their locations, then it makes no difference if someone else shows up with the original tickets. You will never know it. The true disaster actually awaits the patron who knows (or is told by the box office) what the original seats were. If the real tickets show up, the theatre does not want to get into questions of how the ticket holders actually got hold of the tickets.

Look at some possibilities.

The original buyer had her purse stolen, which contained the tickets. It might appear that the new user of the tickets was the thief who stole the purse. Possibly, this could be a matter for the police.

But does your theatre make exchanges? What if the actual thief took the stolen tickets to the box office and exchanged them for another performance? Then another, totally innocent patron bought those same tickets. Neither the box office nor the innocent patron would have any reason to question the transactions at the time. If that occurs, and it can, how could you make a public accusation at a performance that the person in the seats is a purse snatching thief?

On one occasion, a patron reported that her tickets had vanished, though she had last remembered seeing them on her kitchen counter. Fortunately, she knew what the seat locations were. Who was sitting in her seat? Her babysitter.

Some of the newest ticket computer systems actually print the buyer's name right on the ticket. This can help. With a system like that, when a ticket is exchanged, the location is returned to the system, and the original ticket is set aside. Thus, when the location is resold, a new ticket is printed. But does that help? What if the original buyer knows the locations, and the new buyer is holding a ticket with his own name on it?

Form 3-5 is a type of lost ticket form. Enter the date of the performance and the seat locations in question, and the authorization of someone, usually a manager. In particular, note the saving language printed on it, "This location void if another claimant presents the bona fide ticket." That is there to protect the theatre.

The form may be printed on thin cardboard, such as ticket stock. Both halves are given to the patron. The tickets taker keeps one half, the patron keeps the other half.

When more control and security is desired, the forms should be consecutively numbered and stapled into booklets, with carbon paper copies. Both halves of the original are also given to the patron, with a half for the ticket taker, but the carbon remains stapled into the booklet. This provides a permanent record of lost seat locations issued.

LOST TICKET LOCATION	LOST TICKET LOCATION
Name_____	Name_____
Date_____	Date_____
Location_____	Location_____
_____ Authorized by	_____ Authorized by
This location VOID if another person presents the bona fide ticket.	This location VOID if another person presents the bona fide ticket.

Form 3–5

CONCESSIONS

There is a lot of profit to be made from your concession operation if you handle it wisely. The fact is people are willing to spend money on drinks, candy, fancy programs, souvenirs, etc., even after they have spent a lot of money on their tickets. It is often observed that some movie theatres make a greater profit from their candy sales than they do from their admissions. There may be an upper limit to what someone will spend for a large box of candy—but you won't find it.

A Concession Performance Statement (Form 3-6) is used for each performance when any type of front of house sales are done. It is designed to show gross sales, not profit or loss. The top of the form contains standard information to identify the type of show then playing. Of particular importance is the entry for "Attendance." For this number, use the actual count of people present in the audience that night, not the number of tickets distributed. That is, if the box office has sold two hundred tickets, but a snowstorm kept half of the people home, the amount of refreshments sold will be more meaningful when based upon the actual attendance. The ticket takers counting the stubs can provide this number.

Total sale of candy, beverages, and miscellaneous items is based upon inventory before the performance less the inventory remaining after the performance. For example, if you start with one hundred candy bars, and after the performance you have seventy-five bars left, you obviously sold twenty-five. You may either count each type of candy separately, or group by price and then count each price.

Beverages can be tricky. If you are selling prepared drinks, bottles or cans, then counting inventory is easy. But if you are pouring from large bottles or automatic machines, that is not possible. Instead, you can inventory the cups. Just as you would the candy, count the number of cups you have available before the performance, then count them afterwards. The difference is the number of drinks sold. To make much sense of this number, the first time you set up, keep track of the number of drinks poured from one bottle. Be consistent with the amount of ice you put in each cup, and the total number of drinks poured from one bottle will be reasonably consistent. Or practice with water from a used bottle.

Miscellaneous merchandise is handled the same as candy. Count the number of T-shirts or posters or whatever is being sold before the performance and afterwards. The difference is the number sold. You could try to keep track of each item as it is sold, but in the rush of intermission business it really is impossible to keep an accurate count.

For all items, be certain the "start" inventory is the same as the "finish" inventory from the most recent performance.

Sometimes, an item is returned because the candy was stale, or the T-shirt has something wrong with it. Perhaps to placate an unhappy patron, you offered them a drink. These must also be accounted for. Deduct them from the bottom of the statement.

The per capita figure is a very useful piece of information. Divide the gross sales by the actual attendance to determine the average dollar amount spent by each member of the audience. After a period of time you will be able to predict the kind of business you will do for different types of productions. For example, most theatres have found that they will sell more refreshments for a musical than for a heavy drama.

By using this form you have the ability to determine if your sales personnel are accurately accounting for their money. The "Net This Performance" figure, plus the cash on hand before the performance, must equal the amount of money in the box after the performance. Avoid the temptation to use the concession money as a perpetual source of petty cash.

CONCESSION OPERATIONS: FORM 3-7

This is a form prepared only once each week, or other regular accounting period. Whereas the Concession Performance Report (Form 3-6) is designed to show gross sales for each performance, the Concession Operations statement (Form 3-7) is designed to show profit or loss for the week. Here the sales figures are listed for each category of refreshments and merchandise, and the actual money spent in purchasing the product that week is indicated. For any given week, the actual cost of the product sold is not a perfect cost analysis. The system works because over a period of time it evens out, and all costs and sales are reflected.

For example, before opening the theatre you purchase 144 candy bars. The cost of all 144 will be reflected the week the bill is paid. During the first week, the theatre may sell only 100. Thus, (if the candy was sold at cost), the first week would show a financial loss in candy sales. However, the second week, there would be merchandise available to sell—44 candy bars—with no cost involved. Accordingly, there would be profit on all 44 sales. Over the two weeks, all costs and sales are reflected and balance out.

In practice, all merchandise will have a considerable mark up (2, 3, or even 4 times cost), and there will be ongoing purchases. Except possibly for the first week of a season, when all new, fresh merchandise must be purchased, the constant turnover, accompanied by a considerable profit margin, should result in a consistent profit.

By separating categories of sales, such as bar, merchandise, souvenirs, etc., it is easier to determine where the better profit centers are. Payroll and sales taxes, which are not offset directly by sales, also must be factored in. A review of the forms show how all the pieces of this puzzle fit together.

Following the small theatre forms are two agreements for hiring concessionaires. The first (Form 3-8) is an individual employment agreement, when a person is hired to run the concessions for the house. The other (Form 3-9) is a sample agreement between a large theatre and a professional concession company. Last (Form 3-10) is a sample of a monthly report from a professional company, indicating gross sales each week for each category of sales, the theatre's percentage share, referred to here as "rent," and the total amount paid to the theatre.

The Well-Run Theatre

Concession Performance Report

Day _____ Date _____ Time _____

Attraction _____ Attendance _____

Performance No. _____ Week No. _____ Weather _____

Item	Start	Finish	Sold	Price	Amount
Candy:					
Beverages:			Subtotal:		
Miscellaneous:			Subtotal:		
			Subtotal:		

Remarks:	Less Returns & P.R.	( )
	NET THIS PERFORMANCE	
	Previous Total	
	TOTAL TO DATE	
Prepared By	$ Per Capita	

Form 3-6

Concession Operations

Week End _____

Attendance   Attraction

1. Bar	Sales	Bills	4. General Expenses		
Liquor					$
Wine					$
Soft Drinks					
Punch					
			NET		
			5. Payroll		
Total			Staff	$	
Less Bills			Manager	$	
NET			Total	$	
			% Payroll Taxes	$	
			TOTAL		
2. Merchandise	Sales	Bills	6. Sales Taxes		
Candy			% of $	= $	
Recordings			% of $	= $	
Cards			TOTAL		
Coat Check			7. Gross Sales	$	
Opera Glasses			Less Products	(	)
Apparel			Less Payroll	(	)
			Less Taxes	(	)
Total			Less General Expenses (		)
Less Bills			SURPLUS/LOSS	$	
NET			Prior Total	+	
			Total to Date	$	
3. Books & Souvenirs			8. Checkbook		
Sales			Opening Balance	$	
% to Publisher	(	)	Deposits	+	
% to Seller	(	)	Less Bills	(	)
NET			New Balance	$	

Signature _____   Date _____

Form 3-7

Employment Letter for Concession Manager

Dear _____:

This letter is to set forth the terms of your employment by the _____ Theatre Corporation.

It is understood that this letter of Agreement will be for an indefinite time, beginning _____, 19__, and will continue in full force and effect thereafter until either party notifies the other in writing of his or their intention to terminate this Agreement, not later than thirty (30) days prior to the effective date of such termination.

Your title will be Concession Manager.

As Concession Manager, you will be responsible to the General Manager and your duties and responsibilities shall be as determined by the General Manager and the Board of Directors. You will be responsible for all operations customarily required to operate the concessions of the _____ Theatre efficiently and effectively; and will include, but not be limited to, the processing of inventory, staffing and payroll (to be submitted as directed), sales transactions (both wholesale and retail), and supervision of sales by and for visiting attractions. Additionally, you may from time to time provide services for special events held at the _____ Theatre.

The _____ Theatre Corporation will pay you as base compensation, exclusive of benefits, the sum of _____ dollars per week, or commissions as determined by the attached schedule, whichever is higher, for an eight performance week, or pro rata thereof.

It is agreed that where and to the extent possible, you may participate in the health benefits program that may be offered to other employees of the Corporation.

It is understood that your employment may be terminated at any time by the General Manager or Board of Directors for just cause, for which no notice will be required. Layoff due to lack of work will not be considered termination.

If the foregoing correctly reflects the agreement between us, please execute the original of this letter in the space provided and return it to the General Manager.

> Sincerely,
> The_____Theatre Corporation
> By:_____
> Title: _____
> Date:_____

Agreed and Accepted:

_____

Date:_____

Form 3-8

Concession Agreement

AGREEMENT made this ___ day of _____, 19__, between _____
THEATRE Co. and _____ COMPANY (hereinafter called the "Concessionaire"),
having its principle place of business at _____.

WHEREAS the Theatre Co. represents that it is the operator of the _____ Theatre
located at _____, and

WHEREAS the Concessionaire desires to obtain an exclusive license to sell soft drinks,
alcoholic beverages, candy, posters, apparal, librettos and recordings, souvenir books and
other souvenir type merchandise, and to operate the checkroom, or to supervise the sale
of the same, on the following terms and conditions:

   1. The Theatre Co. hereby grants to the Concessionaire the exclusive right to sell soft
drinks, alcoholic beverages, candy, posters, apparal, librettos and recordings, souvenir
books and other souvenir type merchandise therein, and to operate the checkroom, or to
supervise the sale of the same.

   2. This Agreement shall be for a term beginning September 1, 19__ and ending August
31, 19__.

   3. a. In consideration of the license granted herein, the Concessionaire shall
pay to the Theatre Co. the following sums:

      1) _____ percent (_____%) of the gross receipts from the sale of
soft drinks, alcohol beverages, candy, and souvenir books.

      2) _____ percent (_____%) of the gross receipts from the sale of
sheet music, posters, librettos, recordings, and other souvenir type
merchandise.

      3) _____ percent (_____%) of the checkroom revenue received by
the Concessionaire. For the purposes of this Agreement, the term
"checkroom revenue" shall not include any gratuities given to the
individual checkroom employee(s).

     b. For the purposes of this Agreement, "gross receipts" shall mean the total
amount received by the Concessionaire from the sale of items, less sales tax
payments for such sales.

   4. With respect to souvenir merchandise (books, shirts, posters, etc.), such sale will be
supervised by the Concessionaire and the Concessionaire shall receive fifteen percent
(15%) of the gross receipts from such sale. The individual salesperson shall receive twenty
percent (20%) of the gross receipts from such sale.

   5. The Concessionaire shall conduct the various concessions at the Theatre in a quiet,
dignified, sanitary and honest manner. The Concessionaire, his agents, servants, and
employees shall abide by and conform with all of the Theatre Co.'s rules and regulations
relating to the Theatre.

—(more)—

6.   Within twenty (20) days after the last Sunday in each month, the Concessionaire shall submit a statement to the Theatre Co. indicating the gross receipts at the Theatre for such month and shall make payment of all the money due to the Theatre Co. for such monthly period.

7.   The Theatre Co. shall have the right to inspect the Concessionaire's books and records for the purpose of verifying the Concessionaire's gross receipts and royalties on which the Theatre Co.'s share is to be computed pursuant to this Agreement.

8.   The Concessionaire agrees to hold the Corporation harmless against any and all claims that may be made or asserted by anyone purchasing or consuming any product sold by Concessionaire, or where the claim relates to damage of any articles alleged to have been checked with the Concessionaire, or the failure to return same, or relates to the quality of the merchandise sold by the Concessionaire, or relates to the conduct of his personnel, or otherwise. In the event of any legal proceedings being instituted against the Theatre Co. arising out of any such claim, the Concessionaire agrees to defend such proceedings at his own expense and to pay the full amount of any verdict, judgement or recovery that may ultimately be had, together with costs. The Theatre Co. shall fully cooperate with the Concessionaire in defending any such legal proceedings. Nothing in this Agreement shall make the Theatre Co. responsible for the debts or obligations of the Concessionaire.

9.   In the exercise of its right and license, the Concessionaire shall be permitted to maintain refreshment bars and a checkroom in the theatre, the location of each to be determined by mutual agreement. The Theatre Co. shall provide the Concessionaire with storage space at the Theatre for his exclusive use at no cost to the Concessionaire.

10. The Concessionaire shall, at his own expense, obtain all licenses, permits or other authority from any governmental agency required to conduct any business under this license, and the Concessionaire agrees to conform to all the rules, regulations and requirements of such governmental agencies.

11. The Concessionaire will, at his own cost and expense, provide public liability insurance with products and food liability coverage endorsements, and property damage insurance for the benefit of Concessionaire and Theatre Co. covering its patrons, guests and employees, the public and any other person or persons, and workers' compensation insurance in connection with its operation of the concession facilities. With respect to liability insurance, the insurance shall be in the amount of not less than the sum of _____ dollars ($_____) on account of injuries to or death of one person, and the sum of _____ dollars ($_____) on account of injuries to or death of more than one person, and that with   respect to property damage insurance, the insurance shall be in an amount of not less than _____ dollars ($_____) per occurrence and _____ dollars ($_____) in the aggregate.

12. The Concessionaire shall pay all taxes or other expenses based upon wages of his employees, sales and use taxes, and any and all other taxes in connection with the operation of his business and hold the Theatre Co. harmless from any claims arising therefrom.

—(more)—

13. All of Concessionaire's employees in the theatre shall at all times be neatly attired, and be of legal age for the activity undertaken. Concessionaire shall not at any time possess, display, sell nor offer to sell within the theatre any indecent, illegal, immoral, or other improper items.

14. Nothing herein contained shall be deemed to constitute a joint venture or partnership between the parties, and the Theatre Co. shall not be liable for any losses of any kind or nature incurred by the Concessionaire resulting from the operation of this Agreement.

15. The Theatre Co. shall furnish the Concessionaire with garbage removal, electricity and water required for the conduct of his business hereunder, without charge.

16. The selection and scheduling of performances given in the theatre shall be at the sole discretion of the Theatre Co. The Theatre Co. may restrict or cancel any or all concession operations for certain performances, at its sole discretion.

17. The exclusive license granted herein shall not be applicable to a) events that take place in the theatre before one-half hour before scheduled curtain time, nor more than one-quarter hour following the end of a performance; b) performances to which only one group has purchased all publicly available tickets, c) non-first class productions.

18. There shall be no modifications or extensions of this license agreement except by a written instrument, properly signed by the parties hereto. Neither party shall assign this Agreement to any other persons or entity.

IN WITNESS WHEREOF the parties have set their hands and seals the day and year first above written.

_____

_____

_____

_____

Form 3–9

The Well-Run Theatre

Concessionaires Report for _____, 19____

Attraction_____

Week Ending	Alcoholic Beverages %	Soft Drinks %	Check Room %	Books %	Candy %	Recordings %	Posters %
1							
2							
3							
4							
5							
Gross Sales							
Less Tax							
Net Receipts							
Theatre Share							

Total Due Theatre:_____

Form 3-10

Concessionaires Report for **November 30**, 19____

Attraction_____

Week Ending	Alcoholic Beverages 15 %	Soft Drinks 15 %	Check Room 15 %	Books 15 %	Candy 15 %	Recordings 10 %	Posters 60 %
1 11-2	1265.40	504.60	8	25.60	297.85	20.25	—
2 11-9	1313.10	393.60	15	16.60	273.40	24.30	12.50
3 11-16	1091.30	273.60	15	21.20	319.95	39.15	5
4 11-23	1292.70	269.40	21.40	19.60	285.90	47.25	5
5 11-30	1080.90	281.40	25.35	23.60	316.80	33.75	10
Gross Sales	6043.40	1722.60	84.75	106.60	1493.90	164.70	32.50
Less Tax	483.47	137.81	—	—	119.51	13.18	2.60
Net Receipts	5559.93	1584.79	84.75	106.60	1374.39	151.52	29.90
Theatre Share	833.99	237.72	12.71	15.99	206.16	15.15	17.94

Total Due Theatre: $ 1339.66

Form 3-11

Chapter 4
Advertising, Promotion and Programs

The rent has to be paid, so does the telephone bill, the gas bill, the electric bill, the insurance, and the royalties. Consequently, some theatres find the easiest place to reduce expenses is by cutting back on advertising. Unfortunately, that is usually very destructive and counter-productive. When money is tight, it may seem difficult to spend another thousand dollars on promotion, but if that additional thousand dollars brings in an extra thousand and one dollars in ticket revenue, then it is worthwhile to make the investment. In addition to extra ticket sales, there is also likely to be an increase in concession income, as well as the intangible benefit of simply having a larger audience in the house.

Forms 4-1 and 4-2 are complete one week schedules of all advertising and promotion. One of them is strictly for print advertising, the other also includes radio and television. Choose whichever fits your needs. Either way, one form is filled out for each week of the engagement, plus one for each week in which preliminary advertising is done. For a three week engagement, you could easily end up with six or seven pages. Those pages would contain the entire scope of all advertising and promotion done for the attraction. It is advisable to do the entire schedule at the very beginning.

That is not to say that nothing will change. Obviously the nature of the reviews, and an unexpected volume of ticket sales—either way—can affect the advertising budget.

The introductory material at the top of the form sets forth information about the attraction, scheduled opening date, and the week/ending of that form's schedule. The schedule itself is shown in the newspaper section and/or the radio/tv section. Enter the name of the media, and for each day of the week, the size and frequency of the ad. For print advertising, the criteria is number of column inches, for radio or tv, the criteria is number and length of spots. Carry forward the arithmetic, and you have the cost of each day, and the cost of each promotion venue.

Form 4-3 is a summary notice and check list for theatre management and press agents. Once set, management does not usually need to know exactly what type of promotion is running at any particular time. The manager and box office do need to know when the first ad appears, when the box office is supposed to start selling tickets for that show, and so on. The checklist helps insure that nothing falls through the cracks.

From time to time certain public or private media want to photograph or film/videotape something inside your theatre. If you are lucky enough to have television news crews filming your opening night, you must give advance notice to the performers and stage crews of the recording. Form 4-4 is one example. The media should expect to pay for any theatre expenses incurred due to their activity. Having said that, remember that everything is negotiable.

Sometimes an organization wants to film something of their own in your facility, or they want to film something of yours for their own purposes. Never forget that you must keep control over what happens inside your facility. As a general guide, a company doing promotion for non-profit purposes is not charged for filming (Form 4-4). However, if the film is to be used for commercial purposes, the theatre should share in that, or at a minimum be paid a fee for the use of the hall. A very short agreement, such as the one included as Form 4-5, should protect your interests adequately. Possibly you may need a more detailed agreement. In that case, one of the booking contracts might work, depending on the specific facts. Remember that any time recording is done inside the theatre, notice must be given to all affected cast and crew (Form 4-6).

Theatre programs can be just another expense for a theatre, or something that visiting attractions must create for themselves. By selling advertisements in the publication, they can be a source of income to the theatre. As with so much else in the performing arts, the nature of performance programs is highly variable. Styles range from typed and photocopied, to glossy, professionally produced, typeset and printed programs that generate thousands of dollars in advertising.

Enclosed are forms used for the two extremes. One, Form 4-7, is for a small theatre company selling advertising space to local merchants. The other, Form 4-8, is a sample contract between a large house and a professional publisher. Terms of contracts between major houses and large publishers are highly variable, and the sample included is one of the simpler versions that may be created. Depending on the needs of your organization, you may add additional language describing the selection of cover material, editorial content, limitations on advertising permitted, technical details regarding paper stock, ink, and sizes. You may need clauses on liability insurance—to protect the theatre from the publisher and the publisher from the theatre, and so on. Finally, when using a publisher, the range of negotiable rights and fees is extensive. You can agree on fixed weekly, monthly, or yearly fees, percentage of gross advertising revenue, percentage of net profits, fees based upon number of weeks played or number of tickets sold. You may increase the obligations of the publisher by adding special events or children's shows, or reduce the publisher's obligations by limiting requirements for any of the above.

But no matter what kind of agreement you have, it is not worth more than the reliability of the publisher. It is no good having an ironclad contract—and a publisher who has failed to deliver programs for opening night, or the next, or the next.

Finally, another often overlooked source of advertising income can be the sale of ads on the tickets and/or the ticket envelopes. Each is usually done on an exclusive basis for one advertiser, generally for the duration of one full season. As a practical matter, the theatre management need not care how many different restaurants or hotels or whatever advertise there, or for how long their commitment lasts. The theatre does care about reliability, so that enough envelopes are printed so that the theatre never runs out (Form 4-9).

A similar source is to sell advertising on the back of tickets. Many commercial ticket printers, or those companies supplying stock for computer tickets, can add copy to the stock. As with ticket envelopes, contracts are usually exclusive with one advertiser but should be made for a specific number of tickets, e.g. ten thousand tickets. If you pay for computer stock, do not contract for a season, as the season may end before, or after, you run out of tickets.

Advertising Schedule

Attraction _____

First Performance _____

Last Performance _____

PUBLICATIONS

MONTH
DAY
DATE

LINES
INCHES
TOTAL

RATE

TOTALS
Per Publication

PRINTED MATERIALS

Heralds

Window Cards

Two-fers

TOTAL

Approved

Date

TOTAL

Advertising Schedule

Attraction _____

First Performance _____ Last Performance _____

PUBLICATIONS

MONTH DAY DATE										LINES INCHES TOTAL	RATE	TOTALS Per Publication

TOTAL _____

WEEKLY NEWSPAPERS

PAPER	INCHES	COST

RADIO/TV

	Sun	Mon	Tue	Wed	Thu	Fri	Sat	# SPOTS	COST

Signed _____

Date _____

Press Department Notice of Promotion Dates

Attraction_____

Announced with subscription_____

First Mail Order Ad_____

Telephone Sales Begin_____

Box Office Opens On_____

First Public Performance_____

Press Night_____

Form 4–3

Permission to Record in Theatre

Dear _____:

In response to your request, this is to confirm that we have given our consent to your filming/videotaping in the _____ Theatre on _____, 19__.

This consent is given on your assurance that this filming/videotaping/taking photographs is not for commercial use. You agree that in the event this film/tape/photographs is/are later used for commercial purposes, you will negotiate with the _____ Theatre Company for its fair participation in the proceeds of such use, and that no such commercial use will be made until agreement for our participation is completed.

You further assure us that you have all necessary legal rights to film/videotape/photograph on that date and agree that you will pay all costs incidental to the above.

Your signature below will indicate your acceptance of this understanding. Please sign both copies of this letter and return the original to my office.

Sincerely,

_____
Name

_____
Title

Recorder:

_____
_____
_____

Form 4–4

Commercial Use

This will grant television station "_____" and "_____" [Name of TV Show] the right to record videotape of and in the theatre, including employees of the theatre, for possible use in a television program segment. "TV Show" is authorized to use the name of the theatre, the name of the undersigned, the names of our employees, and the above video tape in connection with a program segment on "TV Show". Such use may include promotion of the program or the stations on which it appears, but will not constitute a commercial endorsement.

We agree that we will not refer to "TV Show" or its use of this theatre, its premises or personnel in any publicity, promotion or commercial advertising (including display advertising on our premises).

Sincerely,

Recorder:

_____

_____
Name

_____

_____
Title

_____

_____

Form 4–5

Memorandum

To: Cast and company and all crews
Subject: Recording performance

This is to inform you that television theatre critics with news crews have been invited to videotape portions of this attraction during the opening night performance. Please note that all recording will be done under the guidelines established by all theatrical unions and that this tape will only be used to accompany reviews of the show and other television-publicity purposes.

Form 4–6

Small Program Advertising Agreement

I agree to purchase an advertisement in the 19__-__ _____ Theatre performance programs. I have indicated the size of my advertisement by checking the appropriate size and price below. I understand that I am responsible for providing camera ready copy by the following dates: September 1, November 1, January 2, February 1, and April 1.

Advertising Rates: Total Contract Price for 5 Issues:

____   Full page $

____   One-half page $

____   One-quarter page $

____   Inside cover $

____   Back cover $

____   A check for $_____ is enclosed.

____   A first payment of thirty percent (30%) of the total annual charge is enclosed. Additional payments of thirty percent (30%) each (reflecting a delayed payment premium) will be made no later than September 1, November 1, and January 2.

Name of advertiser_____

Type or brand name of product _____

Representative _____

Address _____

_____

Form 4–7

Contract with Program Publisher

THIS AGREEMENT, made and entered into this _____ day of _____, 19__, by and between the _____ Theatre Corporation, operator of the _____ Theatre, hereinafter sometimes referred to as "Theatre", having its principle office at_____, and _____ Company, hereinafter sometimes referred to as "Publisher", having its principle office at _____.

WHEREAS, Theatre is engaged in the operation of a theatre for performing arts; and

WHEREAS, Theatre desires to distribute house programs of uniform high quality free of charge to each member of audiences attending theatrical performances at the _____ Theatre; and

WHEREAS, Publisher represents that it possesses the necessary experience and resources to publish such programs and can do so in sufficient quantity for such free distribution in the _____ Theatre.

—(more)—

NOW THEREFORE, Theatre and Publisher, mutually covenant and agree upon the following terms, each of which is a condition of this Agreement.

1. TERM OF AGREEMENT: The term of this Agreement shall be for a period of five (5) years, commencing on September 1, 19__, and ending on August 31, 19__, or at the conclusion of any attraction then performing at the _____ Theatre, whichever date is later.

2. OBLIGATIONS AND RIGHTS OF THE THEATRE:

A. Theatre hereby grants to Publisher the exclusive right to publish programs for patrons of performances at the theatre. Theatre agrees to use its best efforts not to permit the distribution for sale or otherwise of any magazine, program or similar material containing advertising of any kind at any of the performances covered by this Agreement. This prohibition may be waived by mutual agreement. Non-program house publications, or souvenir programs, librettos or like materials that may be sold or distributed in other cities for the same attraction may be sold or distributed at the _____ Theatre.

B. Program notes and all information relevant to productions at the theatre and information on the theatre will be provided to Publisher by Theatre before the first performance of the relevant attraction. Publisher will not alter or change program notes or other information provided by Theatre except for correcting grammar, spelling, etc. Any material supplied to Publisher shall be solely and exclusively for its use in producing said programs, and will not be used by Publisher for any other purposes whatsoever, and will be returned to Theatre if requested. Theatre will control the subject matter appearing on the cover of each program, and will supply all cover material camera-ready for each program.

C. Theatre will indemnify Publisher and hold Publisher harmless from any cost or liability whatsoever arising from Publisher's use in these programs of material supplied by Theatre.

D. Theatre will provide program notes and other information and material required for any given period at least ten (10) working days in advance of requested delivery date of programs. In the event Theatre does not provide all material on the time specified in this paragraph, then Theatre will pay to Publisher any incremental costs incurred by Publisher on account of such late submission of materials.

E. This Agreement is subject to cancellation by Theatre for just cause, by written notice to the Publisher no less than eight (8) weeks before such cancellation shall take effect. "Just Cause" may include, but not be limited to, poor program quality, failure to deliver programs on time, failure to deliver sufficient quantities of programs, failure to make any payments due Theatre as specified, or failure to cure any other material defect within forty-five days of written notice thereof. Determination of quality of programs shall be in the sole judgement of Theatre, such judgement not to be unreasonably applied. Notwithstanding the foregoing, failure to deliver programs on time or in sufficient quantities may result in the immediate cancellation of this Agreement, at the Theatre's option.

F. It is understood that from time to time Publisher may request to purchase prime

—(more)—

location seats. Theatre will make best efforts to accommodate such request.

3. OBLIGATIONS AND RIGHTS OF THE PUBLISHER:

A. Publisher agrees to publish and supply to Theatre programs for patrons of performances at the theatre. Publisher shall have the exclusive rights to all revenue that may be derived from advertising that may appear in the program.   Non-program house publications, or souvenir programs, librettos or like materials that may be sold or distributed in other cities for the same attraction may be sold or distributed at the _____ Theatre.

B. Publisher has the authority and discretion to create, design, solicit and accept advertising for programs, except that Publisher shall not print advertising from a competing entertainment without permission from the Theatre.

C. Publisher will own all rights to the program and its contents, except as otherwise provided.

D. Publisher will allow Theatre twenty-five (25%) space of the total content (excluding all 4 covers) for Theatre's own use for program information, background comment or synopsis of the attraction, for biographical material on the performers, and may also include lists of boards of directors, staff lists, donors, etc., house advertising or advertising traded to other legitimate arts organizations, and which may include up to ten (10) black and white halftones within the editorial section of the program. The Theatre will provide photos at its own expense. Theatre (including visiting attractions) retains copyright for all copy and photographs it provides.

Publisher will supply at its expense a standard size program (approximately 5 1/2" wide by 8 1/2" high). The program will be printed on coated stock no less than sixty (60) pounds. The publisher will provide a four-color cover program. The front cover shall contain a photograph of the attraction or of the theatre, at the theatre's discretion. The quality of the programs shall not be less than that of the program sample attached hereto.

E. The program will be printed in quantities as required during each month, depending on the needs of the Theatre. It is understood that the maximum requirement for any four week period will be forty thousand (40,000) copies. Publisher will print half the expected production run for the month, allowing for possible cast changes. Lead time for such changes to facilitate typesetting and printing shall be a minimum of five (5) working days. In the event that Theatre requires changes in less than five (5) working days, Publisher shall use its best efforts to accomplish the same, charging Theatre only the incremental cost incurred therefore. In the event of unexpected major billing changes, Publisher will, at cost to be paid by Theatre, either (a) paste over attraction title page, or (b) provide papers to be inserted into programs by Theatre, containing such new information as necessary. Saturdays, Sundays, and holidays are not included in the term "working days."

F. Publisher will make every effort to accommodate Theatre's wishes and opinions on subject matter and treatment. Copies will be provided by the Publisher to the Theatre for the purpose of proofreading. It is the responsibility of the Theatre or Theatre's agent to

—(more)—

check these copies for accuracy. Author's alterations other than typographical errors, and/ or additions to these copies, will be charged to the Theatre at cost.

G. If Publisher receives the material from Theatre at least ten (10) working days in advance of requested delivery date, Publisher will deliver programs no later than the requested delivery date, except due to circumstances beyond the control of Publisher, such as, but not limited to, acts of God or labor strikes.

H. One program will be distributed to each patron at each performance for which a regular ticket is sold (including discounts and complimentary). Programs will not be made available to audiences at free performances, or for events not open to the general public.

I. Publisher shall produce said programs and deliver them to the Theatre at no cost to Theatre, except as set forth herein.

J. Publisher agrees to pay Theatre _____($). All payments from Publisher to Theatre are to be made not more than thirty (30) days after _____.

K. This Agreement may be canceled by Publisher by written notice to Theatre no less than thirteen (13) weeks before such cancellation shall take effect, in the event that Theatre is consistently late in providing program notes or other material as specified in Paragraph 7 hereof, or failure to cure any material default within forty-five (45) days of written notice thereof.

4. ARBITRATION: Any dispute arising from this Agreement that is unable to be resolved between the parties hereto may be submitted by either party to the American Arbitration Association in accordance with the Voluntary Rules and Regulations for final and binding arbitration. The arbitrator's award may be confirmed in any court of competent jurisdiction. All expenses of the arbitration shall be shared equally by the parties.

5. MODIFICATION: This instrument contains the entire and only agreement between the parties, and no oral statements, representations or extraneous written matter not contained in this instrument shall have any force or effect. This Agreement may be modified only by written agreement of the parties hereto.

6. JURISDICTION: This Agreement shall be governed by the laws of the state of _____.

Theatre Corporation

_____

_____

Publisher

_____

_____

Form 4–8

Agreement to Supply Ticket Envelopes

Dear _____:

This letter will confirm the understanding between us with respect to your furnishing the _____ Theatre with theatre ticket envelopes with your advertising material printed thereon for the one (1) year period beginning September 1, 19__, and ending August 31, 19__.

1.   You agree to furnish theatre ticket envelopes at your sole cost and expense for the _____ Theatre. The envelopes must conform in size, layout and text to the sample envelope attached hereto. Prior to printing you will submit a proof for approval by us.

2.   You will provide five hundred thousand (500,000) envelopes, of which three hundred thousand (300,000) shall be delivered to the Theatre by August 15, 19__, and two hundred thousand (200,000) to be delivered by January 15, 19__. You will provide inside delivery at the theatre.

3.   We agree that the envelopes furnished by you (subject to your satisfactory performance under this agreement) shall be the only envelope authorized to be used by us at the _____ Theatre.

4.   In consideration of our granting you the exclusive right to advertise your copy upon said envelopes, you agree to pay to us the sum of _____ dollars by November 1, 19__.

5. The exclusive use agreement shall be for a term of one (1) year commencing September 1, 19__, and ending August 31, 19__. You shall have the right to extend the term of this agreement for an additional period of one (1) year, provided (a) you give us ninety (90) days notice in writing of your intent to do so and (b) you have fully and faithfully complied with all the terms and conditions in this agreement.

6.   In the event you choose to extend the terms of this agreement for an additional period of one (1) year, the fee shall be increased by fifteen percent (15%), and the number of envelopes to be provided shall be as specified by us.

7.   This agreement may not be changed or altered except by a written agreement between the parties. This agreement may not be assigned to any other person or entity.

For the _____ Theatre Corp.

_____

_____

Accepted by:

_____

_____

Form 4–9

Chapter 5
Theatre Payroll

Community and school theatres generally do not have paid staffs, however, regional and professional theatres do. Even if the payroll is computerized, there are a myriad of forms that can help the manager or bookkeeper keep track of the payroll before it is sent to the computer. Some employees may be on fixed salary, some are not, but either way, time is usually charged against different attractions. As with other theatre operations, there are plenty of possibilities for the unusual or problem case. Several forms are included here that are shortcuts and time savers.

Form 5-1 is a summary cover sheet, indicating by work area the entire payroll for the organization. For these payroll operations, such details as why the employee worked is not included because here, such information is irrelevant. If the person is on your payroll, you must pay him/her, whether or not the theatre is reimbursed by another source. The summary page is only to insure the identification of proper payment of wages to each iindividual, not explain why they are paid. These numbers must correspond with numbers entered on various other reports, particularly the operating statements, but they appear here first. Settlements with attractions may carry different amounts, because not all costs are charged to producers.

The theatre creating this form used its payroll account to pay almost all payroll related bills. Thus, the employer's share of payroll taxes, worker's compensation, and F.I.C.A., as well as the employer's share of health benefits for certain employees, are deposited into the payroll account. Some benefits, generally the union pension and welfare payments, are made directly from the manager's account.

This form is, in effect, an invoice for total payroll costs. The amount of the check to be written is clearly explained and indicated on the bottom of the form. There is a concise, historical record which shows the bookkeeper's account number.

Some employees work regular hourly schedules, somewhat removed from performances or fixed units of time. Office workers (telephone operators, box office employees, stage doormen) can use Form 5-2 to keep track of daily hours and pay. Transfer the bottom line to the summary page.

Ushers (Form 5-3), are usually paid a certain rate per performance. The rate varies depending on whether the usher works only the beginning of the show, or the entire performance. Enter name and amount to be paid for each performance worked, then total. Transfer the bottom line to the summary page. Note that instead of days of the week, the performance is indicated by number. This is convenient for those theatres where the performance schedule varies from week to week.

Musicians' pay involves a number of elements. They get paid for performances and rehearsals, and also for such items as the number of different instruments they play (Form 5-4).

The Well-Run Theatre

Of all employees working in a theatre, those with the most complicated payroll are usually the stagehands. Form 5-5 identifies who worked, and why. For stagehands in particular, why they worked is very important. Stagehands often represent the largest payroll for a theatre operation. All regular union contracts require that stagehands be paid in increments of several hours or by events. That is, a stagehand who arrives at the theatre to work on repairing scenery will be paid for a minimum of, usually, four hours; even if the time actually spent to do the work is less. A performance will be paid either at a fixed performance rate, or at a number of hours per performance, usually 3 1/2 or 4, even if the performance ends much sooner. Of course, if the show is a long one, they will be paid additional time, in increments of one hour "or part thereof."

Consequently, time sheets must be kept in great detail, and still be flexible enough to handle the many activities that occur. Form 5-5 was designed with that goal in mind. Notice the various elements, the name of the attraction, the day and date of the work (or indicate the week ending), and the department, if there are enough employees to call for separate pages.

The names of the individual employees are listed in the left column, with the number of hours worked, together with that employee's hourly rate in the appropriate column. Activities may be mixed on one page, if conditions permit. For example, one day's pay could include a work call, a rehearsal, and a performance. Total the columns down, total individuals across, and the two should balance. Because much of the stagehands' costs are often charged back to the attraction, it is important for the theatre manager to have the written approval of the show's company manager, or stage manager, or the show's department heads. There is room for their signatures at the bottom. (A "department head" is the individual employee in charge of a particular work jurisdiction, such as "head carpenter" or "head electrician.")

At the end of the week, if needed (it usually is), Form 5-6 is filled out, providing a way to keep track of each employee's total earnings for the week. Where there is no vacation pay, or the computer system adds vacation pay automatically, your form might stop with the total of the days, and not have the subtotal or vacation pay columns.

The same forms can be used for wardrobe employees. Alternatively, Form 5-7 is a form showing a combination of hours and performance pay.

Actors, Form 5-8, are different, as they have only performances or rehearsals; however, touring actors also receive a per diem allowance for their meals and lodging. Transportation to and from the city is paid directly by the company. Per diems are paid without deductions of any taxes. Note that according to various union contracts, some pay is determined at 1/6th of weekly salary, while other time is based on 1/7th weekly salary.

Employees working under most union contracts will have health and welfare benefits paid or deducted automatically. However, the organization may have a benefit plan for other employees as well. Where this is optional, there must be a procedure, in writing, to allow the employer to make a deduction from an individual's payroll check. Form 5-9 satisfies this need.

Sometimes an employee reports that his check was lost or stolen. Form 5-10 puts this claim in writing, and protects the theatre, as well as the employee, in case the missing check ever shows up. Form 5-10 is the result of the missing check. Once management has verified the need to reissue the check, or if for any other reason a payroll check is made out of the normal sequence of payroll operations, a "Manual Check Report" should be made and recorded. While regular payroll checks may be prepared by computer, a manual check is prepared by hand, as its name implies. Taxes and other deductions must also be computed manually, and a careful record kept of the process so that all the numbers can be entered into the permanent computer system. Note indication of social security number and number of withholding deductions (married/single, and the number of dependents).

Sometimes people are not taxed. Special consultants and guest speakers are paid fees, not wages. Nevertheless, the I.R.S. is interested in their earnings too. So you must keep a record of what you pay, and report it to the I.R.S. (Form 5-12).

Sometimes emergencies arise and you must contact employees at home, or their next of kin. At the risk of invading someone's privacy, each employee should fill out an emergency contact card (Form 5-13). These are quite easy to handle if they are printed on 5" x 8" file cards, and kept in a special box. Employees should be reminded to keep their cards up to date. This information is confidential and access to these cards should be limited.

Theatre Payroll w/e		
DEPARTMENT	A/C No.	Payment
Box Office		
Manager & Office		
Telephone Clerks		
Group Sales		
Ushers		
Housekeepers		
Stage Doormen		
Actors		
Musicians		
Wardrobe		
Stagehands		
Subtotal		
Payroll Taxes		
Benefits		
TOTAL PAYROLL DEPOSIT		

Form 5-1

The Well-Run Theatre

PERSONNEL REQUIREMENTS

Period From: _____ Through: _____ Department: _____

NAME	JOB DESCRIPTION	MON. From	MON. To	TUES. From	TUES. To	WED. From	WED. To	THURS. From	THURS. To	FRI. From	FRI. To	SAT. From	SAT. To	SUN. From	SUN. To	Total Hours	RATE	TOTAL COST
1.																		
2.																		
3.																		
4.																		
5.																		
6.																		
7.																		
8.																		
9.																		
10.																		
11.																		
12.																		

EXPLANATION:

REQUESTED BY: _____ APPROVED BY: _____ AUTHORIZED BY: _____

Ushers/Ticket Takers Payroll									
w/e_____									
Name	1	2	3	4	5	6	7	8	Total
Totals									

Form 5–3

Musician's Payroll

Attraction_____ w/e_____

Name	Instrument	Base Pay	Rehearsals	Doubles	Misc.	Total
TOTALS:						

Form 5–4

Show:													Day	Date
Dept:														
Employee	Call:			Call:			Call:			Call:			Total	
	Hr.	Rt.	Amt.	Hr.	Rt.	Amt.	Hr.	Rt.	Amt.	Hr.	Rt.	Amt.		

OK _____
Company Department Head

Total

OK _____
House Steward

OK _____
Company Manager

Form 5–5

143

The Well-Run Theatre

NAME	Mon.	Tues.	Wed.	Thurs.	Fri.	Sat.	Sun.	Sub T	Vac.	Total
TOTALS:										

TOTAL EARNINGS

SHOW: W/E:

Form 5-6

THEATRE WEEK _____ / _____ / _____ TO _____ / _____ / 19_____

WARDROBE SHOW:	NAME	MON	TUE	WED	THU	FRI	SAT	SUN	STRAIGHT HRS/SHOW	RATE	AMOUNT	OVERTIME HRS/SHOW	RATE	AMOUNT	TOTALS
															SUB
															%
															TOTAL

JOB STEWARD

WARDROBE SUPERVISOR

Actor's Wages

Performer_____ w/e_____

Social Security No._____ Payroll No_____

Deductions: Federal_____ State_____ City_____

==

Regular salary	_____
Per performance rate	_____
No. of perfs this week	_____
Other	_____
Total performances	_____

Weekly rehearsal salary	_____
Daily at 1/6	_____
Daily at 1/7	_____
No. of days rehearsal	_____
Hourly rate	_____
No. of hours rehearsal	_____
Other	_____
Total rehearsal	_____

Overtime rate	_____
No. of hours overtime	_____
Total overtime	_____

Previous week adjustments _____

Other _____   _____

Other _____   _____

Total adjustments   _____

Total Taxable Wages	_____
Weekly per diem	_____
Daily per diem	_____
Other non-taxable	_____
Total non-taxable	_____

==

Notes:

Form 5–8

Authorization for Deduction of Health Benefits Share

I hereby authorize and direct my employer to deduct from my wages my share of contributions to the Health Benefits Program.

Amount of employee's share as of this date is $_____ or _____%; such amount is subject to change.

Signature_____

Name (print)_____

Address_____

_____

Job (usher, stagehand, etc.)_____

Today's date_____

Form 5–9

Lost Check Certification

I, _____, certify that on _____,
   (print full name)   (date)

my payroll check was lost or stolen. I request that a duplicate check be issued to me. I will cooperate with my employer and the bank in locating the check or otherwise determining what happened to it, and I will cooperate in providing information that may lead to the identification of any person who was responsible for its loss. If the check is cashed, I will, if asked, execute a notarized affidavit of forged signature.

_____
Signature

===
For Office Use Only:

Name on Check_____
Social Security Number_____
Date of Check_____
Amount of Check_____
Check No._____

Form 5-10

Manual Check Report

Employee _____   SS#_____

Address _____   M S 0 1 2 3 4 5 6 7

         _____

         _____

Incorrect pay: $_____

Correct pay: (_____)

This check: $_____

                     Gross pay (this check):   _____

                     Federal Tax   _____

                     FICA   _____

                     State tax   _____

                     Union dues   _____

                     Health benefits   _____

                     Misc.   _____

                     Net Amount This Check   _____

Date requested: _____

Date prepared: _____

Check number: _____

w/e: _____

Approved by:_____

Form 5–11

To:

So that the _____ Theatre may correctly file I.R.S. form 1099, Non-employee's Compensation, for tax purposes, it is necessary that we have your social security number on file. Please fill out the bottom of this form and return it to the Theatre office as soon as possible.

==

Name _____

Address _____

         _____

Social Security Number_____

Signature_____

Form 5-12

Last name_____ (first)_____ (middle)_____

Address_____ (zip) _____

Telephone: Home_____ Date started work at theatre _____

Job at theatre_____

Place of birth_____ Date of birth_____

Social Security Number_____ Marital status_____

In case of emergency please contact:

    Name   _____

    Address   _____

                  _____   PLEASE

    Telephone (h)_____(o)_____   PRINT

    Relationship_____

Today's date_____

Signature_____

Form 5–13

Chapter 6
Theatre Management in the Office

For some reason, many organizations pay less attention to their financial affairs than almost anything else. Most managers deposit money and write checks, and they may know what the bank balance is, but some managers have no real idea whether their theatre is making money or losing money. Some operators cannot tell you which shows made a profit, and which shows lost money. They do not even know how much money they lose when there is no show at all playing in their theatre. These operators insist that profit-loss statements, or operating statements, are something only bookkeepers and accountants care about. But a manager should care.

Having answers to these questions is not difficult. All that is required is a basic system, such as the one that follows. This system walks the operator step by step through the mechanics of tracking expenses and receipts. A management system consisting of a list of bills to be paid, an operating statement, a financial settlement with each attraction, etc., is shown and explained in this chapter. As with the box office, the user can look at the pieces and see how the parts of the puzzle fit together.

A check list of "Permanent Attraction Files" is also included, because the operator must keep permanent files for each attraction, whether produced in house or visiting.

The forms and systems described in this chapter follow a specific operational sequence. Give performances, settle with the producer, and pay bills. While not many professional theatres follow the "traditional" pattern of operations anymore, it is still useful for explanatory purposes to show how to construct the manager's weekly package.

THE TRADITIONAL PRACTICE

Assume a theatre is presenting eight performances each week, Monday through Saturday, with two matinees. The show is an independent attraction, with terms set by a contract negotiated by the theatre and the attraction. The accounting weeks ends Saturday night.

Throughout the week, various bills come from suppliers, vendors and advertisers. Payroll costs are incurred.

After the last performance of the week begins, the theatre manager and the company (attraction) manager decide, according to the terms of the contract, how to split the box office receipts, and how much of the weekly bills and payroll each will pay for. The theatre manager then prepares a type of bookkeeping report called a "settlement" reflecting the distribution of income and expenses. Whichever party owes money to the other—usually the theatre owes money to the show—that manager would then write a check to the other for the amount shown on the settlement. This is all done after the last performance of the week.

By Monday morning, the theatre manager has received a check from the box office account for the week's gross receipts, has written checks to pay bills and payroll, completed an operating statement, balanced the checkbook (as easily done as said) and sent all paperwork to the theatre owner or operator.

Memorandum

To: Theatre manager
Subject: Permanent files

A file is to be established for each and every attraction that performs in the theatre. All information relevant to the attraction is to be filed in this one official file. All presentations, whether performing arts or public service, must have a file.

The official file should contain the following:

1. The booking contract. All presentations, whether performing arts or public service, must have a contract. If the presentation was produced in house, include all memoranda and budgets.

2. All correspondence with the producer or representatives.

3. All ticket orders if the house orders tickets. If the house sells tickets printed by the attraction, include a copy of the ticket transfer information.

4. Original box office statements for all performances for which tickets are sold, whether or not the performance is actually given. Include the box office statements, group sales contracts, complimentary ticket orders, subscription discount reports, and other indicators of discount ticket prices. Actual ticket stubs and deadwood should be stored in another secure location.

5. The manager's weekly package, for every week of the engagement. Include the settlement, the operating statement, the check list, and copies of all bills and payrolls.

6. Advertising schedules, tear sheets, and reviews.

7. One program.

Form 6–1

Memorandum

To: Theatre manager
Subject: Weekly package

The following documents comprise all the weekly reports issued by your office. They should be completed by Monday of each week, and delivered to the General Manager as soon as possible. All of this material goes into the permanent files of the theatre.

a) The settlement with the attraction

b) The operating statement

c) The check list

d) Copies of all bills that were paid, including payroll. Note: for bills charged to the attraction, include the originals in the settlement; for other bills, originals go with the operating statement

e) Carbons of the checks that were written

f) Copies of all deposit slips for the manager's account

g) All box office statements (with all documentation)

Form 6–2

BANK ACCOUNTS

The size of your organization and the general level of activity of your financial transactions will determine the number and types of checking and savings accounts your organization should have.

A very small operation might need only one checking account, with all activity flowing through that account. This works only when box office sales are small, receivables are very low, there is virtually no payroll, and the entire operation is basically hand to mouth.

For larger operations, additional accounts are needed. If there are more than ten people on the payroll, then a separate payroll account should be used. Similarly, if there are more than about eight performances during a month, one or more box office accounts probably will be useful. Still, the nature of box office sales will be relevant.   Is the box office open daily or only before performances? Are there advance sales? Mail orders? Subscriptions? How many days or weeks before a performance is the show on sale? —will also influence that decision.

For major organizations with extensive, long term planning and budgeting, other accounts may be necessary for reserve funds, endowments, etc.

Paradoxically, having numerous accounts actually makes for simplicity in operations. Obviously there are more accounts to balance. Nevertheless, by isolating activities, it is much easier to keep track of those activities. Rather than having "paper" transactions going on, with offsetting deductions and payments, there is evidence that bills were actually paid in full instead of partially, obligations were met, and that what should have happened actually did happen. Separate accounts eliminate more clutter than they create. It is easier for the manager to deal with payroll totals than to plow through an expense list with each individual employee's earnings reported alongside the advertising bills and rent.

Another area that looks complicated but is not has to do with the preparation and style of the checks themselves. Instead of using regular business checks, with a separate stub, use voucher checks with carbon copies. Voucher checks have a large area attached in which you can include useful information, such as the invoice number, the name of the show, the week ending in which it was paid and the type of expense the item is for. Carbons are very useful because even after the check is mailed out, there is a clear record of what each check was for. For the clearest record possible, don't hand write the checks, type them. Voucher checks with carbons are also available for most computer programs.

Following is a detailed description of the basic types of accounts commonly used in performing arts organizations. As noted above, not every company will need every account, some will need few, some will need all of them, and others will need even more specialized accounts. Smaller organizations may combine functions.

About signatures. Many organizations believe that having two individuals sign all checks is a good safeguard for the organization. That may be true for checks that are blatant, obvious fraud, or an extraordinary, obvious waste of money. But that is not often the case. A mere cursory review of a check or invoice is not likely to reveal such a problem. In too many organizations, the second person signing a check merely relies on the first, providing no safeguard whatsoever. In some, a supply of blank, signed checks is kept on hand. Alternatively, enabling a single individual to sign checks clearly establishes that that person is solely responsible for its legitimacy.

For the accounts listed below, the person shown is the individual who would usually prepare the checks written from that account. Others may be on record with the bank to sign checks in the event of illness or emergency.

Manager's Account

All bills directly connected with visiting attractions, settlements, theatre operations expenses, profit checks, and checks covering total payroll and taxes are paid from this account.

Income for this account comes primarily from the box office weekly receipts, advances or deposits from coming attractions, and settlement checks (if applicable) from visiting attractions. This account should zero out or balance out at the end of each week. If profits and losses are covered by use of a general account, all profit for the week is paid to the General Account, while any loss is collected from the General Account. The manager's account balance can start at an arbitrary amount, say, $1.00, and will return to exactly $1.00 at the end of each week. If profits and losses are not covered, then simple arithmetic will indicate, in advance, where the checkbook balance should be after all deposits and checks are prepared.

Any time the balance does not end where it should, then there is a mistake somewhere, the

difference is not merely a change in profit or loss.
Usually signed by: Theatre Manager.

Payroll Account

Only the gross payroll and employer's share of payroll taxes is deposited into this account, the source being the Manager's Account. All net payroll checks are written from this account, as well as all checks where the source of the funds is deducted from the   employees' earnings (e.g., federal income tax withholding, FICA, state and local taxes, union dues, etc.).

This is another zero account. At the end of each pay period, the account should, in theory, return to zero (or one dollar). Because there is no profit or loss involved, there is no reason to have a balance other than zero. However, because tax check payments do not coincide with payroll, there will be some odd balances. Thus, on a weekly basis, the account will not zero out. If this becomes a problem, then a separate account can be opened, and tax payments drawn from the payroll account can be deposited there, until the proper time to send the tax and insurance checks to the proper authority.

Usually signed by: Theatre Manager.

Box Office Account

All money from the sale of tickets, for both current and future performances, are deposited into this account by the box office treasurers, mail order department, etc.

The only checks regularly written from this account include checks paid to the Manager's Account for the exact amount of box office receipts as shown on the box office statement. Separate checks should be written for each separate week or separate attraction. (See Theatre Cash Flow on page 179.)

Also, draw checks to the Manager's account for items such as group sales commissions, sales tax on tickets, and refunds for tickets.

No operating expenses of any kind are covered by this account. Bank charges deducted automatically by the bank should be repaid by the Manager's account and reflected as an office expense of the theatre. Any petty cash borrowed from the box office should be repaid to the box office. The check for ticket sales receipts should always be for the full amount of the box office statement.

This is another zero account. At any given moment, the assets of the account—total money deposited plus money in the cash drawer—should precisely equal the liabilities, tickets already sold. At a time when there are no tickets to sell to a future event, there should be enough money to cover the checks written; there should be no money left over in the account.

If there is a continuing schedule of ongoing performances, then a periodic audit of the box office and this account must be done. (See Chapter 1.)

Usually signed by: Box Office Treasurer.

The Well-Run Theatre

General Account

Expenses from this account may include basic overhead costs, such as utilities, rent, etc., as well as major repairs or purchases. Corporate taxes may be paid from this account. This would be the only account of the basic four (Manager's, Payroll, Box Office, General) that never balances out to zero. Losses from the Manager's Account should be covered by the General Account.

Income includes profit from the Manager's Account, concessions, and unearned income of any type, such as grants and contributions.

Usually signed by: General Manager.

Note: The preceding accounts are the minimum recommended. Other accounts may be established as follows:

Production Account

This account pays for all expenses associated with the production of a show, in those organizations that produce their own shows. Expenses may include scenery, wardrobe (costumes), electrics (lights and sound), and any other costs associated with the creation of individual shows. Depending on the size and activity level of the operation, separate box office (for advance sales), and payroll (for actors and production personnel) accounts may be useful.

Usually signed by: Company Manager.

Number 2 Box Office Account or Advance Sales Account

This account handles most receivables on behalf of the regular Box Office Account. It is responsible for collecting from credit card companies (American Express, Visa, etc.) and paying such amounts to the regular Box Office Account. Most banks charge a higher commission for faster payment, so the organization must decide a) how long it can wait for its money, and b) how much commission it can afford to pay. If the payment delay is much more than a week, then this account does not wait to collect from the credit card banks themselves but instead pays the Box Office before the money is received. Similar procedures are used to handle ticket brokers and agencies.

This is a zero account; however, it is important to note that the cash flow is backwards, that is, funds must usually be paid out before they are deposited in. That means that this account must have an advance float of cash to operate. All organizations, regardless of size, must be prepared to deal with the problems and delays associated with credit card sales.

Usually signed by: Department Head (box office treasurer, head of advance sales, head of subscription, etc.) or Theatre Manager.

Tax Account

This account may be used to pay all payroll taxes, as well as state and/or local sales taxes on tickets. This removes a burden from the General Account or payroll account.

Usually signed by: Theatre Manager or bookkeeper.

Concessions Account

This account is set up to handle the cash flow from theatre concessions. Expenses of purchasing the food, drink, and novelties (e.g. T-shirts) that are sold; and deposits from the sales of these items flow through this account. Any profit or loss goes to the General Account.

This is a zero account.

Usually signed by: Concessionaire.

Savings Account

If the company has significant advance sales for a long running attraction or season subscriptions, it may be worthwhile to open up an interest bearing savings account, or even short term certificates of deposits. Traditionally, interest on such accounts is not shared with the attraction for which the tickets were sold. These funds must be held in escrow until the performances are given. (In the event of a cancellation, refunds must be made.)

Signatures: General Manager.

Capital Improvement Funds, Endowment

Organizations that save money for long term projects, such as building funds or creating an endowment, should establish funds that are isolated from daily operations, and earn interest. Usually, these funds must be tracked and reported on taxes and grant applications.

SETTLEMENT WITH THE ATTRACTION

Whether the attraction is an outside booking, or was produced by your own company, you will have to settle your accounts with the attraction.

The process of settling with an attraction, whether it was produced inside or outside your own organization, is the process of settling the money issues. Generally, by the time of the settlement, the advertising has been run, the scenery has been built, the costumes acquired, the performers paid, and the money collected for the sale of tickets. The act of settling is merely the execution of the contract terms.

To settle, the manager must be very familiar with all the terms of the agreement. He must know virtually every detail about the presentation of the attraction at her theatre. The manager must have assembled all the bills that have anything to do with the presentation of the show and anticipate any other bills that are going to arrive after the show closes. The manager must have all the box office statements and be able to attest that they are correctly prepared. In short, the manager must know the ramifications of every decision made as part of the settlement process.

If the show was produced by another organization, there will be another party, a producer or company manager, to work with in an arms length relationship. Management's dealings with that producer must be governed by the terms of the booking agreement (Chapter 2) signed before the show ever entered the facility. Following the terms of the contract, the manager of the theatre and the manager of the show will have to divide the box office receipts, and determine what advertising each is responsible for. They must settle costs of scenery, payroll for the performers and stage-hands, royalties, and so on. Or, according to the terms of the contract, the theatre pays the producer, or the producer pays the theatre, a flat rate for presenting the show.

At the end of the week it is time to actually apply the financial terms of the agreement. It is quite common for costs to be incurred that were not expressly determined by the contract. For example, suppose the producer agreed to pay for all advertising and promotion costs. However, promotional handouts arrive without any local information printed on them, so the theatre imprints the flyers with the name of the theatre and the performance dates. The fact that the theatre did it does not alter the terms of the agreement. When you settle with the show, bill the producer for the money spent on his behalf.

Continuing with this example, assume by the terms of agreement the theatre pays the producer a flat fee of $5,000 for the week, which includes all advertising. However, if you spent $1,000 for printing those flyers—which is an advertising cost—instead of giving the producer $5,000, deduct the printing costs, and give the producer the net check, or $4,000. But take note: if you spend money on the producer's behalf, get his specific approval in advance.

Some organizations produce their own shows, so there is no third party to deal with. Unfortunately, a feeling often develops between the individuals involved with the show and the regular theatre management that "we're on the same side, why are you fighting with me?" Nevertheless, it is wise to establish a procedure that accomplishes the same effect as the arm's length relationship. The effect gained, when "settling" within the organization, is to isolate costs directly attributable to the specific attraction. Of course one always needs to account for fixed costs and overhead of the organization, but that may be accounted for in another manner (see section on Operating Statements later in this chapter). Expenses such as royalties, advertising, construction or purchase of scenery and costumes, and performance payroll (which would include all artistic talent, as well as most back-stage and front of house employees) should be charged to the show and kept separate from regular, permanent staff (managers, bookkeepers, stage doormen, receptionists, security, and so on).

As with so many of the forms and methods described in this book, the style of what is shown is less important than the process used to accomplish the same purpose. What follows are forms that compose a reliable, easy to use system for settling the attraction.

GENERAL NOTES ABOUT SETTLEMENTS

The week ending (usually shortened to "w/e") of the attraction is the accounting period for the production. Most theatres operate on a weekly basis. The choice of time is yours to make, but should not be casually changed. That would cause inconsistency in comparative results. There is no law requiring a weekly settlement with the producer, but doing so every week reduces errors, helps avoid forgetful memories, provides cash flow and access to funds, etc.

When settling with a Producer, there are two major elements of the settlement: the division of the box office receipts and the distribution of production bills.

First, the box office receipts. These are the net receipts actually shown on the bottom line of the box office statements. The Theatre share is determined by the terms of the contract. For example, when the theatre and the show split the ticket sales equally, it is reflected there. Receipts times theatre percentage equals house share, and receipts times show percentage equals attraction share. The two shares added together must equal the total box office receipts:

> Box office receipts: 2,700.00
> Theatre share (50%)   (1,350.00)
> Attraction share (50%)   1,350.00

Sometimes the percentage changes with the gross receipts, e.g., "the house receives 100% of the first $50,000, 0% between $50,000 and $125,000, and 50% of all receipts over $125,000." When this happens, figure out the actual shares on another paper, and just show the actual shares on the settlement. (Be sure to keep a copy of your formula.) Sample: Gross receipts = $133,000.00: 100% of $50,000 = $50,000; + 0% of $75,000 = 0; + 50% of $8,000 = $4,000; so total house share = $54,000:

> Box office receipts: $133,000.00
> Theatre share: (54,000.00)
> Attraction share: 79,000.00

If the theatre pays the attraction a fixed fee for presenting the show, only that fee need be shown, as the box office receipts are not shared. Example: Attraction Fee: $1,000.00. For a fixed fee, it is usually not necessary to give the producer a copy of the box office statement.

Second, distribute production bills. The theatre manager assembles the weekly bills and makes the first determination as to which bills are the responsibility of the producer and which are the responsibility of the theatre. Depending on the contract, there may be many expenses that can be charged to the show, or none at all. This can only be determined by a review of the contract, and should not be subject to negotiation or arbitrary decision making at the time of settlement.

From the attraction share, subtract the cost of any expenses that the theatre has paid, but are, according to the contract, the actual responsibility of the attraction. The difference between the attraction's share less the bills charged against it, is the amount the theatre owes to the producer:

> Box office receipts: 2,700.00
> Theatre share   (1,350.00)
> Attraction share   1,350.00
>
> Attraction bills: (450.00)
> Amount due attraction: 900.00

Bills charged to the show could include anything. The only guide the manager has is the written contract. Here is where arguments arise. Sometimes the theatre charges the attraction for an expense, but the producer insists that the expense was not authorized or required by the contract. For example, consider the earlier example where the producer is responsible for advertising and promotion. The theatre charges for printing flyers with the theatre's name, address and the dates of the show on them. But the producer balks, saying he never approved that item, and it was not necessary for the presentation of the attraction. Who requested the flyers? Why? Only the principles can decide what is correct.

The Well-Run Theatre

Even when distribution of costs is not at issue, advertising presents special problems because of the size and ongoing nature of the expense. There are several different approaches to handling charges. If bills for advertising and promotion arrive before the end of the first week of the attraction, you can save them until that first week and charge them all at once. This puts a big expense in the first week, and may easily cause a net loss to be shown.

For example: A show is scheduled for four weeks. In the four weeks preceding opening, $250 per week is spent promoting advance sales. It also spends $250 weekly promoting the show during the first three of those four weeks. No advertising is scheduled during the fourth week, assuming it may be sold out by then. Total advertising expense: $1,750.

Week -4	$ 250
Week -3	250
Week -2	250
Week -1	250
Week 1	250
Week 2	250
Week 3	250
Week 4	0
	─────
Total	$1,750

Costs could be reported each week as they are incurred. That means showing an expense during either a dark week, or during the previous attraction. Neither way makes sense. A better way is to hold those costs until the show opens, placing the expense where it belongs, with the show it promoted.

But there is still a decision to make. By the time of the first week of the attraction, there has been $1,000 in preliminary costs, and $250 in current expenses, or $1,250 of the total budget of $1,750. Then, the second and third week of the show only report $250 each week, and nothing for the closing week.

Week 1	$1,250
Week 2	250
Week 3	250
Week 4	0
	─────
Total	$1,750

To charge 71% of the advertising budget to 25% of the show can be a severe jolt to the system, and is not an accurate representation of the cost of promoting ticket sales for each week. A more accurate reflection of cost per ticket is to amortize the costs of that preliminary advertising. Divide the preliminary promotion expense by the number of weeks of the engagement, in this case four, or $250 per week. Each week report one share of the amortized expense, in addition to the current expense.

	Prelim	Current	Total
Week 1	$ 250	250	500
Week 2	250	250	500
Week 3	250	250	500
Week 4	250	0	250
Totals:	1,000	750	$1,750

While this is a more accurate representation of the expense, placing it where the value is found, it does not present a true portrayal of when costs were incurred. Also, advertisers generally expect their bills paid in full weekly.

This problem can be solved by paying media bills when they are due, but amortizing the costs to the attraction. This is done by billing the attraction at an amortized rate, paying the bills when they are due, and showing a "due from attraction" (a minus) on the check list (see section on "Check List" later in this chapter). Each week report the expense as if paid weekly, but without a new check number. It will be a "received from attraction" credit. While this sounds complicated, it is quite workable.

NOT ENOUGH MONEY TO GO AROUND

What happens if the show has run up more bills than its share of receipts? There are a number of ways to handle that problem.

If the show is playing for more than one week, then the "debt" often can be carried forward to the next week. In the second week, box office sales are likely to be higher, and expenses are likely to be lower. The previous week's "debt" can be added in to the second week's bills. (For purposes of this example, assume receipts did not change, and all bills were charged in the first week.)

1st Week:	Attraction share:	1,350.00
	Attraction bills:	(1,500.00)
	Amount due theatre:	150.00

2nd Week:	Attraction share:	1,350.00
	Attraction bills:	(150.00)
	Amount due attraction	1,200.00

Note that the "Amount due theatre" is not actually paid when due.

If the show is closing, the theatre operator must find a way to insure payment. Depending on the relationship between the theatre operator and the producer, this may mean trusting the producer to pay as soon as he can. Or it may mean threatening—or taking—legal action against him, or just not letting him remove his scenery from the theatre.

SETTLEMENT FORMS

Form 6-3 is a style of settlement suggested by the preceding examples. It clearly indicates such factors as box office receipts, each party's share, and expenses that are charged to the attraction according to the contract. Attached to this page would be additional information that shows clearly how each of the expenses was determined, and includes supporting information, such as payrolls and invoices from the media for advertising.

Form 6-4 is a completely different kind of settlement. This is usable when the attraction is paying virtually all the house expenses, all payroll, all advertising, all overhead, and even the rent. Form 6-5 reflects the same costs as shown in 6-3.

SETTLEMENTS WITH YOUR OWN PRODUCTION

In most organizations, when the company produces its own shows, there is no contract outlining the terms of the engagement. Nevertheless, doing the paper work that has the same effect as settling with the show creates a record for each individual attraction. There are certain differences. Since there is only one organization, the box office receipts are not split up. Instead credit 100% of the box office receipts to the show, but also bill 100% of the costs to the show:

Box office receipts:	2,700.00
Attraction bills:	(2,600.00)
Balance:	100.00

The organization still keeps the balance. The balance is the profit from the show; but of course it does not indicate whether the organization made any money for the time spent in the theatre, if rent and other overhead are taken into account.

Should rent and overhead be charged to the attraction? That is a matter of philosophy. Many managers think it should—directors and producers think it shouldn't. Arguments against charging overhead are that doing so hides the actual cost of an attraction. That is, if a play is produced two years in a row, but in the second year the rent on the theatre has increased $1,000.00 per month, is it fair to suggest that the second year the company spent that much more on the production?

On the other hand, charging rent imposes some realism on directors and producers. Extended periods of rehearsal and scenery construction can tie up a theatre and keep it from being used for income generating performances. Without rent charges a show may appear to have made a profit, but would look quite different if the theatre also lost several thousand dollars while sitting dark during rehearsals.

It is possible for an attraction to make money, while the organization loses it. In either case, all costs of operating the theatre should be reflected on the weekly operating statement.

Settlement

_____ Theatre

"Hamlet"
w/e April 27, _____

Gross Receipts:	$ 45,507.03
Theatre Share (25%):	(11,376.76)
Company Share (75%):	34,130.27
Company Expenses:	(10,713.14)
Amount due Company:	$ 23,417.13)

Company Expenses

Stagehands - Take In & Rehearsals	3,254.89
Stagehands - Performances	1,970.40
Wardrobe	785.92
Advertising	3,461.51
Telephone Service	25.47
General Expenses	1,214.95
	_____
Total Expenses:	$10,713.14

Approved:

For the Company:

For the Theatre:

Form 6–3

Weekly Settlement of Receipts and Expenses

Attraction_____ w/e_____

COMPANY EXPENSES

PAYROLL		GENERAL EXPENSES	
Manager	_____	Electricity	_____
Office	_____	Gas	_____
Press	_____	Water	_____
Group sales	_____	Insurance	_____
Box office	_____	Taxes	_____
Ushers	_____	Telephones	_____
Phone operators	_____	Legal/Acct	_____
Musicians	_____	Rent	_____
Stagehands	_____	Box office	_____
Wardrobe	_____	Repairs	_____
Stagedoor	_____	Departmental	_____
Engineer	_____	Equipment	_____
_____	_____	Booking fees	_____
_____	_____	Office	_____
		Print ads	_____
TOTAL PAYROLL	_____	Radio & TV	_____
		Printing	_____
		Signs & photos	_____
		P.R.	_____
PAYROLL TAXES & BENEFITS		Delivery	_____
F.I.C.A.	_____	Postage	_____
ATPAM Pension	_____	_____	_____
ATPAM Welfare	_____	_____	_____
Office Health	_____	_____	_____
Box Office Health	_____	_____	_____
Musicians Health	_____		
Musicians Pension	_____	TOTAL	_____
Stagehand Pension	_____		
Stagehand Welfare	_____		
Stagehand Annuity	_____	TOTAL SALES	_____
Wardrobe Pension	_____	House share	(_____)
Wardrobe Welfare	_____	Payroll	(_____)
_____	_____	Taxes/benefits	(_____)
_____	_____	Expenses	(_____)
_____	_____	_____	(_____)
TOTAL	_____	Amount due.	
		Theatre	_____
		Company	_____

Approved:

Company Manager_____   Theatre Manager_____

Form 6–4

Weekly Settlement of Receipts and Expenses

Attraction __Hamlet_____ w/e _April 27, 19___

COMPANY EXPENSES

PAYROLL		GENERAL EXPENSES	
Manager	_____	Electricity	_____
Office	_____	Gas	_____
Press	_____	Water	_____
Group sales	_____	Insurance	_____
Box office	_____	Taxes	_____
Ushers	_____	Telephones	25.47
Phone operators	_____	Legal/Acct	_____
Musicians	_____	Rent	_____
Stagehands	5225.29	Box office	_____
Wardrobe	785.92	Repairs	_____
Stagedoor	_____	Departmental	1214.95
Engineer	_____	Equipment	_____
____	_____	Booking fees	_____
____	_____	Office	_____
		Print ads	3461.51
TOTAL PAYROLL	6011.21	Radio & TV	_____
		Printing	_____
		Signs & photos	_____
		P.R.	_____
PAYROLL TAXES & BENEFITS		Delivery	_____
F.I.C.A.	_____	Postage	_____
ATPAM Pension	_____	____	_____
ATPAM Welfare	_____	____	_____
Office Health	_____	____	_____
Box Office Health	_____	____	_____
Musicians Health	_____		
Musicians Pension	_____	TOTAL	4701.93
Stagehand Pension	_____		
Stagehand Welfare	_____		
Stagehand Annuity	_____	TOTAL SALES	45,507.03
Wardrobe Pension	_____	House Share	(11,376.76)
Wardrobe Welfare	_____	Payroll	(6,011.21)
____	_____	Taxes/benefits	(_____)
____	_____	Expenses	(4,701.93)
____	_____		(_____)
TOTAL	_____	Amount due Theatre Company	23,417.13

Approved:

Company Manager_____

Theatre Manager_____

The Well-Run Theatre

Sooner or later, someone will ask, "Are we making any money?" A manager will appear more competent if he can provide a serious answer, rather than just looking at the floor and shuffling his feet. True, many groups keep track of whether individual shows make or lose money. And at the end of a fiscal year they probably know their financial position. But many people believe current details are hard to figure out.

A group may report that its last show made a $1,500 profit. But what happens to that profit if the theatre pays $2,000 per month rent, and was closed for one month while the show rehearsed and built scenery, and then took the next four weeks to gross enough to make that $1,500 "profit"? Is the rent figured into that "profit" anywhere? What about other expenses, such as heat, water, and electricity? Are the salaries of regular staff included in the cost of the show?

What about advertising? If $4,000 is spent to advertise a four-week show, when should bills be accounted for? It is easy to see that the average weekly expense for advertising is $1,000, but what if all the money were paid in the first week? Or if none of it were paid until the show closed?

What about bills that arrive before a show opens? If another show is playing, do you report all advertising bills when they arrive? That would double the apparent cost of the advertising for the current show. If the theatre were closed, should advertising be an expense when the theatre is dark?

In addition to finding answers to these questions, a good system will make it possible to see where money is going, and how to explain losses. A good system will make it possible to compare accurately the costs of one show with another, and the costs of running the theatre from one year to the next.

Finally, a good system provides a permanent record for the organization. It will be possible months or years later to study what was done at any given time, to see why things went well, or with the benefit of hindsight, where mistakes were made. Some granting organizations now require such accurate information.

The system described here forms a significant part of a "package" of materials that comprise the official record for the theatre. The package includes settlements, operating statements, and paid bills. The system can be easily adapted to local conditions without breaking the ties that bind the pieces together. For example, if an organization reports on a monthly basis, rather than weekly, a change to monthly reports does not change in any significant way what is shown here.

Like many aspects of theatre management, utilizing a unified system of accounting is easy to do, but offers a myriad of ways to make mistakes. Fortunately, with the systems described here, most mistakes rise to the surface, so that they can be corrected sooner, rather than later.

SYSTEM OVERVIEW

With the system described here, a manager will account for all of the theatre's income and all of the bills that are paid, during a regular, fixed period of time. Each element of income and expense is analyzed and reported on an operating statement. The "bottom line" of an operating statement is the profit or loss for the accounting period. All the paperwork can be assembled in one place at one time, and becomes part of the permanent records of the organization.

OPERATING STATEMENTS

All forms of operating statements work in a similar manner. While each organization has certain items peculiar to it, in general, the biggest differences are only in the layout and design. The operating statement should reflect all financial activity in the theatre for one week (or month, or possibly from the end of one attraction to the end of the next). The statement lists all the expenses incurred at the theatre during the week, regardless of whether the theatre will be reimbursed for the expense. All credits and reimbursements from the show are deducted from the total costs. The differences between the expenses and the credits, together with the box office receipts and the settlement with the attraction, is the profit or loss for the theatre for that week. The operating statement should be balanced against a list of checks written, in order to be certain everything was included and no mistakes have been made.

Note that on the operating statement, the amount of the check itself does not matter. For example, if one check includes $200 for printing flyers for the show and $50 to print box office forms, $200 is shown in the advertising section, and $50 is shown under general expenses. For all operating statements, the following guidelines apply:

PAYROLL

Be sure to list all wages paid. The work of some employees, such as technicians, stagehands, or musicians, may be separated by the work actually done (e.g., rehearsals, performances, etc.), and by the attraction the work is done for. Reimbursements are determined by the settlements with the attractions. Be certain to include payroll taxes and benefits where appropriate. Determine the net cost for each section. On some forms, payroll benefits and taxes may be included in each section. On others, the separate sections only include wages paid, with a separate section for benefits and taxes.

ADVERTISING

The advertising section includes a) all advertising bills actually paid by the theatre, b) all radio, television, and other media bills, c) promotional printing and postage, and d) all other public relations bills, such as some ticket refunds, opening night parties, etc.

GENERAL EXPENSES

General expenses include a) all general expenses listed on the settlement, b) repairs and maintenance, either actually incurred or a fixed amount to be accumulated for major expenses, c) rent, d) utilities, e) equipment rental and purchases, f) office expenses, printing forms, supplies, coffee, g) telephone service, h) tickets, i) etc. Most of these expenses are strictly house costs, and are not usually reimbursed by visiting attractions.

A fee paid to the attraction for the show itself is not a general expense. It may be shown either as a production expense, or as a share of box office receipts, deducted from the box office receipts on the settlement.

There is another way to handle certain general expenses. Instead of charging a full month's rent in one week, a major repair cost, the large expense of buying new equipment, or a lump sum insurance premium, deduct a pro rata weekly portion of these expenses. Determine the total annual amount of all of these charges, then divide by 52. Each week charge a single "overhead" expense of 1/52 for those items included. This way, the rent is accounted for every week, whether a show is playing or not. Also, it provides a reliable way of saving up enough money to actually pay those bills when they become due. (The important concept here is to save.) A check for an overhead cost could be paid each week to the organization's general account.

Whether you pay overhead weekly, or charge individual current costs, it all will be charged against profits, sooner or later.

OPERATING STATEMENT FORMS

Included here are several styles and types of operating statements. They include two styles for theatres with paid employees ("professional"), and two styles for organizations with volunteer staff ("non-professional," amateur, community or academic). All of them follow the general rules set forth above, but present information in varying ways. These may be used right out of this book, or adapted to the specific needs of your organization.

Form 6-6 is a fairly simple form used in a professional theatre. The payroll information is reasonably detailed, providing information on all departments.

Payroll taxes and benefits are shown separately. To be sure, benefits, and even taxes, could be shown combined with salaries in the earlier sections. However, the process of figuring actual payroll for individuals is somewhat removed from figuring benefits that are paid to unions or insurance companies. By separating the benefits, it is easier to keep track of those expenses in an orderly manner. A variation on this theme would be to show benefits combined by type, instead of by employee group. That is, instead of showing all stagehands' benefits as one cost, all the pension fund contributions could be shown on one line, with all the health benefit fund contributions on another line, and so on. Local conditions will suggest the best method for individual organizations.

General expenses are fairly obvious, with all advertising and promotion, and overhead included.

Note that for all of these categories, there is a place to indicate credits from the attraction. These are the same numbers that appear on the settlements with the shows. The total of "Less Credits" must equal the total "Company Expenses" charged on the settlement.

The "Total Net Gross" is the bottom line from the box office statement, the Company Share is off the settlement, as is the House Share. As is the case with all operating statements, the bills paid, (including attraction bills) plus or minus the profit/loss, must equal the box office receipts.

Form 6-7 is also an operating statement for a professional theatre. This differs from Form 6-6 in that it is more detailed. Not more complicated to fill out, only more detailed. The distribution of stagehands costs is clearly set forth, as they are for musicians and wardrobe. Advertising is greatly expanded. Another expanded area on this form is the Box Office Receipts section. The gross receipts for each performance is indicated, as well as room for other income the organization may have received.

The advantage of this form is that more detail is presented. A sample of Form 6-7, filled out in summary fashion, is included. The particular amounts match up with the sample check list, Form 6-12, and the cash flow, page 179.

Form 6-9 is a form for a community theatre. This form is similar to that of Form 6-7 in that it presents much detail for the ongoing operations of the organization. Several of the groups list theatre expenses as on the other forms. But this statement is for an organization with many activities, such as workshops. Note how distinctions are made for income from isolated activities. That is, the section on workshops is independently complete. The workshop expenses are shown, but so is the income from participants. Thus, actual net profit or loss is instantly determined. Concessions is operated completely in house, and can be examined the same way, providing quick recognition of the value of the operation.

Note also the detail for general expenses, broken further into "institutional" and "overhead". The entire payroll for the company, never amounting to more than two or three people a week, is contained in the single line item, "staff." Sometimes a lot of detail is not necessary.

Take special note of the Gross Receipts block. The theatre clearly presents shows only on weekends, but has numerous sources of other income, including credits from a government source, that pays bills for the company, but never transfers money to the company.

Next (Form 6-10) is an operating statement used by an organization to keep track of activities other than its regular theatre operations. Here, the other activities are much more extensive and varied. Some of these other activities produce income, some do not. This organization sponsored lunchtime symposia, special children's shows on Saturday mornings, a play reading library, and an extensive fund raising department. Another temporary department was "construction," used during an expansion of the facility. (Actual construction costs were kept separate.) While this particular form is very specialized for one organization, it provides a good sample for addressing certain needs of community based organizations. For example, if the theatre also operated some form of visual art gallery, such activity could easily be shown as one of the departments.

A final word on the bottom line profit or loss. Theatres of all types rely heavily on grants, contributions, and other unearned income. Each organization must decide for itself how to reflect this income. For example, the bottom line may reflect what actually happened in terms of ability to cover expenses, with contributions added to lessen the impact of the loss. Or the income may be reflected as income and credits, so that the bottom line suggests that the company operated within predictions or budget. Either way, the final accounting should be the same.

The Well-Run Theatre

Weekly Operating Statement

Attraction_____ w/e_____

PAYROLL		GENERAL EXPENSES	
Manager	_____	Utilities	_____
Office	_____	Insurance	_____
Press	_____	Rent	_____
Group sales	_____	Maintenance	_____
Box office	_____	Departmental	_____
Ushers	_____	Booking fees	_____
Phone operators	_____	Office	_____
Musicians	_____	Advertising	_____
Stagehands	_____	_____	_____
Wardrobe	_____	_____	_____
Stagedoor	_____	_____	_____
Engineer	_____	_____	_____
_____	_____	Total expenses	_____
_____	_____	Less credits	(_____)
		Net expenses	_____
Total Payroll	_____		
Less Credits	(_____)		
Net Payroll	_____	TOTAL SALES	_____
		Company Share	(_____)
PAYROLL TAXES & BENEFITS		House Share	_____
F.I.C.A.	_____		
ATPAM	_____	Payrolls	_____
Office	_____	T & B	_____
B.O.	_____	Expenses	_____
Musicians	_____		
Stagehands	_____	Net expenses	_____
Wardrobe	_____		
_____	_____	SURPLUS (LOSS)_____	
Total T & B	_____		
Less credits	(_____)		
Net T & B	_____		

==

Approved:

Theatre Manager_____ General Manager_____

Form 6–6

Statement No._____ Attraction_____

Week of Engagement_____ Week Ending_____

RECEIPTS				# FRONT OF HOUSE SALARIES				# ADVERTISING		
MON	M			HOUSE MANAGER				PRINT MEDIA		
	E			BOX OFFICE STAFF				RADIO & TELEVISION		
TUES	M			USHERS				MECHANICAL & PROD. CHGS.		
	E			STAGEDOOR				SIGNS/BILLS/PHOTOS		
WED	M			FIREMEN				PRINTING		
	E			HOUSEKEEPING				PUBLIC RELATIONS		
THU	M			MAINTENANCE				MAILING & POSTAGE		
	E							DELIVERY		
FRI	M									
	E			FICA TAXES						
SAT	M			FRINGE BENEFITS						
	E			TOTAL						
SUN	M			LESS CREDITS				TOTAL		
	E			NET FRNT OF HOUSE SALARIES				LESS CREDITS		
								NET ADVERTISING EXPENSES		
				# STAGEHAND SALARIES						
				CARPENTRY DEPARTMENT				# GENERAL EXPENSES		
NET BOX OFFICE RECEIPTS				PROPERTIES DEPARTMENT				TICKETS		
LESS COMPANY SHARE				ELECTRICS DEPARTMENT				REPAIRS & MAINTENANCE		
THEATRE SHARE				TAKE IN				OFFICE & BOX OFF. EXPENSES		
REHEARSAL RENTALS				TAKE OUT				DEPARTMENTAL EXPENSES		
THEATRE RENTALS				REHEARSALS				INSTRUMENT RENTAL & TUNING		
TOTAL THEATRE RECEIPTS				PERFORMANCES				EQUIPMENT RENTAL		
				MAINTENANCE CALLS				I.B.O. CHARGES		
								USHERS EXPENSE		
# PRODUCTION SALARIES								OVERHEAD		
				FICA TAXES						
				FRINGE BENEFITS						
				TOTAL						
FICA TAXES				LESS CREDITS						
PENSION				NET SHAGEHAND SALARIES						
WELFARE								TOTAL		
WORK. COMP.				# WARDROBE SALARIES				LESS CREDITS		
UNEMPLOYMENT								NET GENERAL EXPENSES		
TOTAL										
LESS CREDITS								NET EXPENSE SUMMARY		
NET PRODUCTION SALARIES				FICA TAXES				PRODUCTION SALARIES		
				FRINGE BENEFITS				PRODUCTION EXPENSES		
				TOTAL				FRONT OF HOUSE SALARIES		
				LESS CREDITS				STAGEHAND SALARIES		
# PRODUCTION EXPENSES				NET WARDROBE SALARIES				WARDROBE SALARIES		
								MUSICIANS SALARIES		
ROYALTIES & FEES				# MUSICIANS SALARIES				ADVERTISING EXPENSES		
PRODUCTION EXPENSES				REG. ORCHESTRA				GENERAL EXPENSES		
PRODUCTION FEES								TOTAL EXPENSES		
COMPANY FEES										
				REHEARSALS						
								RECAPITUALTION		
								TOTAL THEATRE RECEIPTS		
				FICA TAXES				LESS NET EXPENSES		
TOTAL				FRINGE BENEFITS				NET SURPLUS		
LESS CREDITS				TOTAL				NET LOSS		
NET PRODUCTION EXPENSES				LESS CREDITS						
				NET MUSICIANS SALARIES						

REMARKS

GENERAL MANAGER: MANAGER:

Form 6-7

The Well-Run Theatre

Statement No._____ Attraction_____

Week of Engagement_____ Week Ending_____

RECEIPTS

MON	M		
	E		
TUES	M		
	E		
WED	M		
	E		
THU	M		
	E		
FRI	M		
	E	6000	00
SAT	M	3500	00
	E	5000	00
SUN	M		
	E		

NET BOX OFFICE RECEIPTS	14,500	00
LESS COMPANY SHARE	4250	00
THEATRE SHARE	10,250	00
REHEARSAL RENTALS		
THEATRE RENTALS		
TOTAL THEATRE RECEIPTS	10,250	00

PRODUCTION SALARIES

FICA TAXES		
PENSION		
WELFARE		
WORK. COMP		
UNEMPLOYMENT		
TOTAL	-0-	
LESS CREDITS		
NET PRODUCTION SALARIES		

PRODUCTION EXPENSES

ROYALTIES & FEES		
PRODUCTION EXPENSES		
PRODUCTION FEES		
COMPANY FEES	2000	00
TOTAL	2000	00
LESS CREDITS	-0-	
NET PRODUCTION EXPENSES	2000	00

FRONT OF HOUSE SALARIES

HOUSE MANAGER		
BOX OFFICE STAFF		
USHERS		
STAGEDOOR		
FIREMEN		
HOUSEKEEPING		
MAINTENANCE		
FICA TAXES		
FRINGE BENEFITS		
TOTAL	1000	00
LESS CREDITS	—	
NET FRNT OF HOUSE SALARIES	1000	00

STAGEHAND SALARIES

CARPENTRY DEPARTMENT		
PROPERTIES DEPARTMENT		
ELECTRICS DEPARTMENT		
TAKE IN		
TAKE OUT		
REHEARSALS		
PERFORMANCES		
MAINTENANCE CALLS		
FICA TAXES		
FRINGE BENEFITS		
TOTAL	2000	00
LESS CREDITS		
NET SHAGEHAND SALARIES		

WARDROBE SALARIES

FICA TAXES		
FRINGE BENEFITS		
TOTAL		
LESS CREDITS		
NET WARDROBE SALARIES		

MUSICIANS SALARIES

REG. ORCHESTRA		
REHEARSALS		
FICA TAXES		
FRINGE BENEFITS		
TOTAL		
LESS CREDITS		
NET MUSICIANS SALARIES		

ADVERTISING

PRINT MEDIA		
RADIO & TELEVISION		
MECHANICAL & PROD. CHGS.		
SIGNS/BILLS/PHOTOS		
PRINTING		
PUBLIC RELATIONS		
MAILING & POSTAGE		
DELIVERY		
TOTAL	1500	00
LESS CREDITS		
NET ADVERTISING EXPENSES	1500	00

GENERAL EXPENSES

TICKETS		
REPAIRS & MAINTENANCE		
OFFICE & BOX OFF. EXPENSES		
DEPARTMENTAL EXPENSES		
INSTRUMENT RENTAL & TUNING		
EQUIPMENT RENTAL		
I.B.O. CHARGES		
USHERS EXPENSE		
OVERHEAD		
TOTAL	2500	00
LESS CREDITS		
NET GENERAL EXPENSES	2500	00

NET EXPENSE SUMMARY

PRODUCTION SALARIES		
PRODUCTION EXPENSES	2000	00
FRONT OF HOUSE SALARIES	1000	00
STAGEHAND SALARIES	2000	00
WARDROBE SALARIES		
MUSICIANS SALARIES		
ADVERTISING EXPENSES	1500	00
GENERAL EXPENSES	2500	00
TOTAL EXPENSES	9000	00

RECAPITUALTION

TOTAL THEATRE RECEIPTS	10,250	00
LESS NET EXPENSES	9000	00
NET SURPLUS	1250	00
NET LOSS		

REMARKS

GENERAL MANAGER: MANAGER:

Form 6-8

Community Theatre Operating Statement

Statement No._____   Week Ending_____

Week of Attraction_____   Attraction_____

FRONT OF HOUSE				GROSS RECEIPTS		
Tickets				Fri. Eve.		
Programs				Sat. Mat.		
Housekeeping				Sat. Eve.		
				Sun. Mat.		
A) TOTAL				Sun. Eve.		
PRODUCTION				TOTAL SALES		
Props				- Attraction Share		
Lumber & Paint				Net Theatre Share		
Electric				+ Rentals		
Royalties				+ Workshops		
Scripts				+ Concessions		
Wardrobe				+ Memberships		
Make-up				+ Gifts & Grants		
				+ _____		
B) TOTAL				G) Total Deposits		
				+ Credits		
PROMOTION				H) TOTAL CREDITS		
Advertising						
Printing				OVERHEAD		
Production				Rent		
Mailing				Gas		
Public Relations				Electricity		
Galas				Alarm		
Photographs				Water		
Displays				Telephone		
				Insurance		
C) TOTAL				Repairs & Maintenance		
INSTITUTIONAL				I) TOTAL		
Office Supplies						
Staff				NET EXPENSE SUMMARY		
Promotion				A) Front of House		
Fundraising				B) Production		
Audit				C) Promotion		
Equipment				D) Institutional		
				E) Workshops		
D) TOTAL				F) Concessions		
				I) Overhead		
WORKSHOPS				TOTAL EXPENSES		
Fees						
Production				RECAPITULATION		
Promotion				H) Total Credits		
				Total Expenses		
E) TOTAL				NET SURPLUS		
- Income				NET LOSS		
Surplus (Loss)						
				RECONCILLIATION		
CONCESSIONS				Opening Balance		
Inventory				+ Deposits (G)		
Production				- Checks Written		
Promotion				Closing Balance		
				+ Accounts Receivable		
F) TOTAL				- Accounts Payable		
- Sales Income				PROJECTED BALANCE		
Net Surplus (Loss)						

Notes

Prepared by_____   Date_____

Form 6-9

The Well-Run Theatre

Cash Disbursements During_____, 19___			
#1 General Staff		**#5 Morning Concerts**	
Staff		Producer's Fees	
Secretarial		Production Costs	
Consulting & Travel		Promotion Expenses	
Legal		Labor Expenses	
Accounting			
Insurance			
Office Expenses			
Repairs & Maintenance		Total	
Telephone		Less Credits	
Prior Months		Net Morning Concerts	
		# 6 Development	
		Special Events	
Total		Public Relations	
Less Credits		Photographs	
Net General Expenses		Labor Expenses	
#2 Lecture Series		Total	
Producer's Fees		Less Credits	
Production Costs		Net Development Costs	
Promotion Expenses			
Labor Expenses		**#7 Construction**	
		Consulting	
		Photography	
Total			
Less Credits			
Net Lecture Series			
		Total	
#3 Children's Shows		Less Credits	
Producer's Fee		Net Construction Expenses	
Production Costs			
Promotion Expenses		Disbursement Summary	
Labor Expenses		Total Expenses	
		Less Credits	
		Total Net Disbursements	
Total			
Less Credits		Remarks	
Net "Children's" Costs			
#4 Gallery			
Total		Prepared by Date	
Less Credits			
Net Gallery			

Form 6-10

ACCOUNTS PAYABLE CHECK LIST

The checklist is the easiest form in this book, and is the keystone of the entire manager's weekly package. This one form, which may be as simple as a sheet of notebook paper with extra lines drawn on it, shows the entire week's activity handled by the manager's account. The list shows every separate, individual bill that is paid by identifying the name of the recipient, the amount of the check, and the check number. The total income for the week is also shown, and when the total bills are subtracted from the income, the profit or loss on the week is determined. That profit or loss must be the same amount previously determined on the operating statement.

If the operating statement is completed before any checks are written, or deposits made, you can predict with 100 percent accuracy what the checkbook balance will be when you have finished the week. Alternatively, if all the bills are paid, and deposits made before an operating statement is completed, you can still determine the profit or loss on the week with 100 percent accuracy. Assuming, of course, what you have done is accurate.

If you did not write the check, or did not make the deposit, the information is not part of the record. You may report only what actually occurred. If petty cash was spent, the petty cash source should be reimbursed by a check from the manager's account, (which can be cashed at the box office). Indicate voided checks so that the check number is accounted for. Show every check and deposit individually. If one check includes payment for more than one bill, just show the total amount of the check on the checklist. If a single bill was paid by two or more checks, report each separate check. Similarly, if box office receipts were deposited in two or more parts, show the amount on each individual deposit slip.

All income from every source should be reported, either directly or indirectly. Include all ticket sales, for all attractions (separate entries for different shows). If there is a separate box office account, show on the check list only the transfer of funds from the box office account to the manager's account. Do not show every daily box office deposit.

Also, list rental income for rehearsal rooms, fees for recording in theatre, and prepayments for future attractions. Some of this income will show up not as profit for the week, but as a credit against future expense.

Note that on an operating statement expenses are grouped according to type of expense—production expenses, advertising, etc. If the bills are shown on the checklist in the same general order, it makes finding mistakes much easier.

If the payroll account is separate, show the total amount written to that account, not the names of individuals being paid. (This list shows checks written from the manager's account, individual payroll checks come from the payroll account.) Remember to show the settlement check written to the attraction, a check received from the attraction for rent or booking fees is reported as income.

The checklist need not show why or on who's behalf a bill is paid. If there is a dispute with the attraction over who is ultimately responsible for the cost of a bill, that is a settlement dispute and is irrelevant to this list. Pay the vendor, report the check paid, and if reimbursed later, report it as income.

The Well-Run Theatre

If an attraction owes money at the end of the week, at the bottom of the list of checks, indicate the source of the debt and the amount in parenthesis. This amount will then be deducted from the gross expense side of the ledger.

The very last number on the check side of the list is the profit or (loss) for the week. Again, this amount equals the amount reported on the operating statement. To balance the account at the end of a week, a loss can be made up by a check from the general account, and shown as a deposit.

Add the entire column of checks written, the profit or loss, and any notes (e.g., an amount due theatre) in that column. The total checks column, and the total of the deposits made, absolutely must be equal, to the penny. If there is so much as a penny difference, there is an error that must be found and corrected.

Form 6-12 is a sample, condensed hypothetical list for the theatre week set forth in the section "Where does the money go?" and the Operating Statement at Form 6-7. For that week, overhead expenses (rent, insurance, etc.) are shown as two payments, and all advertising expenses are also shown as one check. Of course, in reality those departments would probably need numerous checks written to pay all the expenses incurred. Nevertheless, for the sake of simplicity, only the categories are shown.

The two settlement checks are listed first. The Friday show performed for a fixed fee ($2,000), while the Saturday attraction performed for a percentage of the gross (50% of $8,500 = $4,250). Because this theatre has a separate payroll account, the manager's account writes one check to cover the total payroll cost, which can include the employer's share of payroll taxes (F.I.C.A., unemployment insurance, etc.). The names of individuals paid do not appear here.

As previously explained, overhead and advertising are shown here as single checks. The total bills paid: $13,250.00

Income for the week totals $14,500, $6,000 from the Friday performances, and $8,500 from the two Saturday performances. Because there were two separate attractions, with two separate booking contracts and settlements, the box office should issue separate checks to cover the total gross receipts for each attraction. If there is only one attraction, then only one check need be written, not one for each performance.

The surplus is shown as $1,250. Total expenses plus surplus equals $14,500; total income is $14,500. The two figures are perfectly balanced.

The surplus must be the same amount that appears on the completed weekly operating statement (Form 6-8).

Alternatively, if there was a loss, the theatre's own operation will determine how to present the loss. If the loss is held in the manager's account, then indicate the loss as a number in parentheses, subtract it from the total bills, and the resulting amount should still equal the deposits. If there is a general account that will cover losses (and receive profits), then a loss covered should be indicated as a deposit. Thus, the deposits will still equal the checks written.

Check List

Attraction_____ w/e_____

Payee	Amount	Ck No	Income

Form 6–11

The Well-Run Theatre

	Check List			
Attraction_____ w/e_____				
Payee	Amount	Ck No		Income
Friday Producer	2000.00	101		6000.00
Saturday Producer	4250.00	102		8500.00
Payroll a/c	3000.00	103		14,500.00
Advertising	1500.00	104		
Rent	500.00	105		
Other Expenses	2000.00	106		
	13,250.00			
General a/c	1250.00	107		
	14,500.00			

Form 6–12

THEATRE CASH FLOW

The following is a simplified spreadsheet of the cash flow for a small theatre for one operating week, showing how the money flows in and out of the various checking accounts. It is not intended to be a "form" that you would fill out weekly. Instead, it is shown to provide the big picture to many of the forms included earlier—box office statements, payrolls, attraction settlements, weekly operating statements, and so on.

Deposits are indicated in plain numbers, checks written out of an account carry a minus (-) indicator.

The week begins with ticket income being deposited into the box office account. On Friday, the box office receipts show $6,000 gross, which is transferred to the manager's account. (See spreadsheet: "$6,000" from "BO a/c" (box office account), "6,000" into "mgr a/c" (manager's account).

There were two separate attractions. The first played one performance on Friday night and grossed $6,000. The other show played two performances on Saturday and grossed $3,500 at the matinee and $5,000 at the evening performance.

The Friday show charged a fee of $2,000 for its one performance. The Saturday attraction agreed to perform for 50% of the gross receipts. 50% of $8,500 = $4,250.

On Monday, the theatre transferred $3,000 to the payroll account, paid $4,000 in regular expenses for the week (such as overhead, advertising, etc.), and transferred $1,250 to the General Account as profit for the week. The payroll for the week was $3,000, paid on Wednesday.

DAY:	B.O. Statement	B.O. a/c	Mgr a/c	Show a/c	Payroll	Gen a/c
Monday		1,000				
Tuesday		1,500				
Wednesday		2,000				
Thursday		2,000				
Friday		3,500				
	[6,000]	-6,000	6,000			
			-2,000	2,000		
Sat Mat	[3,500]					
Sat Eve	[5,000]					
Saturday		4,500				
		-8,500	8,500			
			-4,250	4,250		
Monday			-3,000		3,000	
			-4,000			
			-1,250			1,250
Tuesday						
Wednesday					-3,000	
	———	———	———	———	———	———
	[14,500]	-0-	-0-	6,250	-0-	1,250

The Well-Run Theatre

The numbers across the bottom of this chart do not add up. Where did the money go?

The box office statements show total sales for three performances of $14,500. The box office account deposited $14,500 from ticket sales and wrote checks totalling $14,500.

The manager's account deposited $14,500 from the box office and wrote checks totalling $14,500.

The two shows received fees and shares totalling $6,250.

The payroll account deposited $3,000 from the manager, and wrote payroll checks for $3,000.

The General Account received a profit check from the manager for $1,250.

Received from ticket sales:	$14,500
General expenses paid to vendors	(4,000)
2 Settlements with shows	(6,250)
Payroll checks to employees	(3,000)
Profit for week	(1,250)

-0-

Chapter 7
Theatre Safety

— Sparks from a malfunctioning light caused a fire to start on the frayed edge of a drop. The flames spread to the loft, which was filled with other drops. The ceiling over the stage rapidly became a roaring furnace, even though the theatre fireman tried to extinguish the blaze with fire extinguishers. After seeing pieces of burning scenery fall onto the stage, the audience rushed for the exits. While no doors were actually locked, some exits were covered by curtains, others were frozen shut. The asbestos curtain was lowered, but hung up on a piece of scenery several feet above the stage. Someone opened a door backstage, and a draft of air blew hot gasses and smoke under the curtain towards the audience. Over 600 people perished, some dying right in their seats.

— Iroquois Theatre, Chicago, 1903

Don't ever think this can't happen in your theatre. While the frequency of theatre fires has substantially declined since the turn of the century, it is clear that fires in places of assembly continue to occur. The rarity of them never excuses their occurrence. The eternal confidence of many people that "disasters may happen to others, but not to me," is all too pervasive in an industry that knows how to prevent, or contain, fires in a theatre.

If you ignore a problem, it does not go away. If it becomes a disaster, you may go to jail. A theatre manager must constantly be aware of fire safety procedures, not only for his theatre, but also for any visiting attractions.

For touring shows, scenic designers have their scenery "flameproofed" when it is constructed by a first class scene shop in New York. Stage managers confidently show their certificate to theatre managers all over the country when the show is on tour. But flame proofing treatment is not permanent, and must be renewed periodically. In many theatres, local managers, and even local fire department inspectors may recognize the certificate as proof of something safe. In fact, the certificate is only proof of a historical event. The certificate cannot indicate the current condition and adequacy of the flameproofing effectiveness.

A manager can establish credibility effectively for fire safety by rejecting outright the offer of the scene shop's flame proofing certificate. Instead, the manager should call the local fire department inspectors, and ask them to conduct an on site test of the scenery, right there on stage. The procedure in one city is as follows:

The fire marshall takes a lighted match, and holds the flame into an edge of a piece of scenery for ten seconds. He then moves the flame away. If the scenic piece holds its own flame for more than ten seconds, the scenery has to be re-treated with flame proofing chemicals. The inspector then moves around the stage, testing virtually every piece of scenery used on stage, or hung from the grid.

Note: Do not do this yourself on material that is obviously, or even possibly, highly flammable. The test used by the fire department in your city may be different. If this test is used, be sure to have a good fire extinguisher next to the tester.

If the scenery, or any piece of it fails this simple test, the remedy is severe. The show does not go on until each and every piece of scenery has been retreated, under the supervision of the theatre staff or the fire department, and retested until it passes. The theatre must have available all necessary equipment and chemicals to do the job. This expense should be charged to the attraction. Note, the fine print in the booking contract must require producers to provide scenery that meets local requirements. New York City standards are good, but by the time the show gets to you, the protections made in that city may have deteriorated.

One of the most important things a manager can do is to develop a strong reputation for being strict about fire safety. Once you do, shows are more likely to arrive in good condition. Of course, it is better for everyone if you test the scenery as soon as it comes off the truck, rather than waiting until right before opening night.

Theatre managers must also uphold their reputation for other safety procedures in the theatre. A routine for safety inspections and awareness must be established. The forms that follow involve two separate, but related aspects of theatre safety. The first is fire safety, the other is general hazards. For each of these forms, the theatre staff should review the listed items, then test their own facility. The lists are not all-inclusive, but they highlight typical problems found in places of assembly. The theatre staff can learn the kind of problems and conditions that arise and must be corrected. The problems are generally universal, and do not vary under local conditions. A tripping hazard in New York is a tripping hazard in Iowa.

As "an ounce of prevention is worth a pound of cure", it is almost always better for the staff to discover its own problems before building inspectors or an accident prone patron does, so that corrections can be made in a manner best for the organization. Management must never delay repairs or improvements to safety defects due to finances or inconvenience. When a fire inspector discovers a hazard, the hazard may make it necessary to close the theatre until corrected. There is no excuse for a theatre operator permitting conditions to deteriorate to that level. If you cannot afford to keep your theatre safe, perhaps you should not be open to the public.

Form 7-1 is a Fire Inspection Guide for Theatres, based on one developed by the office of fire prevention in a municipal fire department. It contains instructions to an inspector on what to look for and check, and what repairs or corrective action is necessary.

Form 7-2 is a sample memorandum to the theatre operator after a thorough inspection has been made of the theatre building. Note that many of the problems listed are not fire defects, but involve other threats to the safety of patrons, performers or staff. Note how calmly the memorandum is written, but take note of the enormous liability on the theatre if any of these defects remain uncorrected, causing a person to sustain an injury.

Form 7-3 is to help with the inevitable. Over time, someone will trip and fall, or hit a thumb with a hammer, or worse. This Accident Report helps record important information at the time the incident occurs.

Forms 7-4 and 7-5 address a fact of life for any public place with high visibility. There are a lot of nuts running around today, and a theatre may be an attractive target of their wrath. When a controversial show is playing (remember how outrageous "Hair" was in the late 1960s?), the possibilities of a bomb threat increase. If the show is politically or religiously controversial, all threats must be taken seriously.

The Bomb Threat Information sheet provides instructions to the staff employee who receives a telephoned threat, and a list of questions that can help authorities determine what to do about it.

The Letter Bomb Information memo, Form 7-5, also provides instructions for the theatre staff, and what to do if something is questionable.

Fire Inspection Guide for Theatres

1. Note the location of fire alarm box nearest to stage door for immediate transmission of fire alarm.

2. Fire alarm box on stage must be maintained in proper working order at all times.

3. Inspect all emergency exits, stairways, alleys and passageways to determine conditions, and availability for use.

4. Examine operation of fire curtain.

5. Examine all automatic fire doors to determine operative condition.

6. Inspect all portions of standpipe and sprinkler systems, including pumps and tanks, and all fire appliances to determine condition and readiness for immediate use.

7. Report unserviceable standpipe or sprinkler systems.

8. Examine automatic skylight to determine operative condition and readiness for use.

9. Inspect all parts of theatre, particularly backstage and under the stage for accumulations of rubbish, and keep clean at all times.

10. Require all doors in proscenium wall to be kept closed during performances.

11. Prohibit smoking in all portions of backstage, under the stage, in dressing rooms, and all other rooms or spaces near stage.

12. Require necessary fire extinguisher to be readily available when materials of a hazardous nature are used in the performance.

(—more—)

---

13. Designate a responsible person to be prepared at all times to take a position in front of the audience to prevent any undue excitement or possible panic condition in the event of an emergency.

14. During each performance inspect all portions of auditorium. Note any obstruction in aisles or passageways or violations of law relative to standees, and take immediate corrective actions when violations are found.

15. At conclusion of performance, require stage trap doors closed and stage elevators made flush with stage floor.

16. Air conditioning system fresh air intakes are to be kept clear of rubbish and combustible materials at all times.

17. Check inspection tags on all fire extinguishers for current valid date.

CORRECTIVE ACTIONS REQUIRED

1. Provide/refill/recharge fire extinguishers located at_____.

2. Provide illuminated "EXIT" signs over doors at _____.

3. Install "NO SMOKING" signs at _____.

4. Remove all accumulations of flammable rubbish from _____.

5. Provide _____ (number) properly covered fireproof receptacles for flammable rubbish at_____.

6. Reduce height of stored materials to not more than eighteen inches below ceiling sprinklers.

7. Discontinue storage, and remove volatile flammable liquids.

8. Discontinue use of open flame.

9. Maintain floors clean of waste oils.

10. Maintain adequate aisle space of not less than _____ inches at _____.

11. Remove all obstructions in front of exit doors at _____.

12. Remove grease, paint, or other accumulation from air ducts at _____.

13. Replace missing or damaged hose on standpipe at _____.

14. Remove all obstructions to sprinkler control valve.

15. Seal sprinkler control valves in open position with approved seals.

16. Remove unapproved iron bars, grill, gates, or other obstructing devices on any windows giving access to fire escapes or to a required secondary means of exit.

17. Require that door of (circle all appropriate) public halls / maintenance room / dumbwaiter / boiler room / laundry chute / incinerator room / kitchen / garage / stairway / storage room be kept closed / be self closing / repaired.

18. Repair lights in stairway at _____.

(—more—)

19. Properly scrape and repaint the fire escape at _____.

20. Store paint and paint supplies in approved storage container or room.

21. Replace used / damaged / missing sprinkler head at _____.

22. Discontinue use of temporary wiring at _____.

23. Provide an affidavit from a licensed fuel oil service company that oil burner is clean and in good operating condition.

Form 7–1

MEMORANDUM

To: Theatre manager
Subject: General safety

A detailed inspection of the theatre facility has disclosed the following problems. It is important that each and every problem be corrected as soon as possible.

Overall:
1. During a simulated power failure, the emergency lighting system did not work at all.

2. Virtually none of the fire extinguishers carry up to date inspection tags. Some are empty, few are where they should be for emergency use, and many theatre areas do not have any fire extinguisher near by.

Lobbies:
3. Carpeting in the lobbies is loose and not flat, creating potential tripping hazard. It must be stretched by carpet installers.

4. There are insufficient ashtrays located in the lobbies.

5. There is an unused refrigerator outside the women's rest room. It must be removed or sealed shut.

6. There is no government permit to sell food (concessions) of any type.

7. The internal communication/telephone intercom system is not working between the lobby and back stage or stage door.

Auditorium:
8. The emergency exit from the rear left of the auditorium opens onto a turning, sloping path. Portions of the safety bannister preventing people from exiting straight has rusted away, which could permit people to push through the bannister and fall off the side of the ramp to the paved area below.

9. Some internal exit signs provide inadequate illumination or are inoperative.

10. Portions of the auditorium and stage are used for construction of scenery, storage of scenic elements, paint, properties, and costumes. This may be against building codes for places of assembly. There are tripping hazards, and many hazardous items could be attractive to children.

11. Regular housekeeping and disposal of rubbish must be improved.

(—more—)

12. The edges of all stairs in the auditorium and backstage must have their edges painted white. Where the stairs are carpeted, white plastic edges should be installed.

13. Loose wires from the back of the sound console located at the rear of the auditorium are a tripping hazard.

Stage:
14. The wooden bannister protecting the stairway on stage left is broken, with a middle rail missing. The bannister is barely attached to the wall, so a person falling against it might cause it to break away, letting the person fall into the stairway.

15. The roof leaks in several places, including directly over the stage dimmer boards. There is a potential problem if any water actually reaches electrical equipment.

16. Because the building was not originally built as a theatre, stage wiring has been inadequately installed and increased over the years. The entire electrical system of the theatre facility should be reviewed by a qualified electrician.

17. Scenery in the current show is stored against the down left wall on stage, causing difficulty reaching the control for the asbestos curtain. This scenery must be moved elsewhere.

18. Combustible wastes are not promptly disposed, but are stored backstage, some in non-metal containers.

19. Some backstage heat vents are blocked by scenery.

20. Numerous common electrical outlets backstage are over loaded and over fused.

21. Some temporary wiring is improper for the electrical load it is carrying.

22. Electrical outlet box on stage right has a cover missing.

23. There is evidence of smoking backstage.

24. The "No Smoking" sign for the stage door lobby is missing.

25. Stage furniture is blocking the up left exit door from the stage.

26. Scenery is blocking the down left standpipe control.

27. All scenery, props or electrics hung over stage or in house, regardless of how small or light should have no less than two (2) lines attached to it, each line being strong enough to singly hold the entire weight.

Dressing Rooms:
28. Anti-slip tape or bath mats should be installed in the dressing room showers.

29. The naked light bulbs in the shower rooms should be properly enclosed.

Stage Basement:
30. The floor mat leading into the orchestra pit from the stage basement is too wide for the doorway; it is turned up at the corners and creates a tripping hazard.

31. Housekeeping should be improved in the stage basement.

(—more—)

32. The drain pipe which runs across the floor in the stage basement creates a tripping hazard.

Exterior:

33. A drain plug located in the floor outside the stage door entrance creates a tripping hazard.

34. Guardrails on all exterior fire escapes are only thirty inches high. They should be increased to forty-two inches high.

35. A trash compactor located under the fire escapes should be moved so that it no longer blocks the lowering of the fire escape ladder.

36. One of the exterior exit lights does not work. The problem could be wiring or the socket, but it is not a burned out light bulb.

37. Parking lot lights are broken in several places. These must be repaired, if not by the landlord, then by the theatre.

During Performances:

38. Stacks of unused programs are left in aisles, causing potential tripping or slipping hazards.

39. Patrons may not sit on stairs in balconies.

40. Crutches of disabled patron may not be left in aisle, causing a tripping hazard.

41. Some ushers inside house do not have working flashlights.

42. Wires for temporary sound effect left loose in aisle.

43. Ushers are sitting in portable chairs placed in front of exits.

44. Recording crew allowed to set up equipment directly in front of rear exit.

45. Fire exit is blocked from the outside.

Form 7–2

Accident Report

Date of Incident_____ Time_____

Event or Performance_____

Location of Incident_____

_____

Name_____

Address_____

_____

Age or Birth Date_____ Telephone_____

Events of Incident_____

_____

_____

_____

_____

Description of injury or property damaged_____

_____

Witnesses: Name_____ Telephone_____

Address_____

Name_____ Telephone_____

Address_____

Police_____

Physician/Nurse/Emergency_____

_____

This report by_____ Date_____

Form 7–3

Bomb Threat

PLACE THIS UNDER TELEPHONE	CALLER'S VOICE

BE CALM, BE COURTEOUS, LISTEN, DO NOT INTERRUPT.

TIME CALL RECEIVED	TIME CALL ENDED

QUESTIONS TO ASK

1. WHEN IN BOMB GOING TO EXPLODE?

2. WHERE IS IT RIGHT NOW?

3. WHAT DOES IT LOOK LIKE?

4. WHAT KIND OF BOMB IS IT?

5. WHAT WILL CAUSE IT TO EXPLODE?

6. DID YOU PLACE THE BOMB?

7. WHY?

8. WHAT IS YOUR NAME?

9. WHAT IS YOUR ADDRESS?

10. ARE YOU CALLING FROM A PAY PHONE?
    ☐ YES   ☐ NO

11. LOCATION AND/OR NUMBER

SEX OF CALLER	RACE OF CALLER	AGE OF CALLER

☐ M ☐ F

EXACT WORDING OF THREAT

CALLER'S VOICE

☐ CALM   ☐ ANGRY   ☐ EXCITED
☐ SLOW   ☐ RAPID   ☐ SOFT
☐ LOUD   ☐ LAUGHTER ☐ CRYING
☐ NORMAL   ☐ DISTINCT ☐ SLURRED
☐ NASAL   ☐ STUTTER   ☐ LISP
☐ RASPY   ☐ DEEP   ☐ RAGGED
☐ CLEARING THROAT   ☐ DEEP BREATHING
☐ CRACKING VOICE   ☐ DISGUISED
☐ ACCENT   ☐ FAMILIAR

IF VOICE IS FAMILIAR, WHO DID IT SOUND LIKE?

BACKGROUND SOUNDS

☐ STREET NOISES   ☐ CROCKERY   ☐ VOICES
☐ PA SYSTEM   ☐ MUSIC   ☐ HOUSE NOISES
☐ MOTOR   ☐ OFFICE MACHINERY
☐ FACTORY MACHINERY   ☐ ANIMAL NOISES
☐ CLEAR   ☐ STATIC   ☐ LOCAL
☐ LONG DISTANCE   ☐ BOOTH

OTHER

THREAT LANGUAGE

☐ WELL SPOKEN (EDUCATED)   ☐ FOUL
☐ IRRATIONAL   ☐ INCOHERENT   ☐ TAPED
☐ MESSAGE READ BY THREAT MAKER

REMARKS

DATE

NAME OF PERSON RECEIVING CALL

NUMBER CALL RECEIVED AT	REPORT CALL IMMEDIATELY TO	TITLE	HOME PHONE

Form 7-4

Memorandum

To: All Staff
Subject: Letter Bombs

This is to notify all staff of the possible dangers of "letter bombs" and ways to recognize them. This is not meant to frighten, but only to raise your awareness, particularly during the next few weeks when our next, highly controversial attraction, is playing.

Be alert for the following:

1. Weight: If in an envelope, the object will seem too heavy for the size of the envelope.

2. Stiff: The envelope will always seem stiff.

3. Address: The address may be incorrect or unusual.

4. Postage: The postage may be incorrect.

5. Return Address: Usually no return address.

Remember that such items may be delivered by courier services and messengers.

If a suspicious item is received, check with the addressee to see if such an item is expected.

A suspicious item must not be opened. Notify postal authorities or the local police or fire department. While letter bombs usually present no danger until opened, they should be handled as little as possible.

Form 7–5

Conclusion

Managing a theatre involves many business, organizational and technical skills; but above all, it involves people skills. On any given day a manager has to deal with the artist, the producer, the patron, the stagehand, the ticket seller, the cleaning staff and the board of directors.

The following are some thoughts to keep in mind when dealing with those worst of all possible days.

1. Stay calm. Getting shows in and out of a theatre involves intensive hard work for a relatively short time. Remember that this show will end, things will quiet down, and life will be back to normal—until the next show.

2. Set the tone. Whether dealing with staff or patrons, the good theatre manager controls the tone. Cooperation or confrontation will depend in large part on the manager's attitude and actions.

3. Listen to your employees. Listen to your patrons. Many difficult situations can be eliminated just by listening to people's concerns. Sometimes the mere fact that you listen attentively will solve the problem, and no other action is required. Where there is a real problem, listening carefully will lead to an agreeable resolution.

4. Solve problems, don't create them. Research the situation as carefully as possible, and then do something.

5. Be flexible. There is a reason for every clause in a contract, every rule and every policy; but there are also circumstances that call for modifying those rules. Enforce rules, but be reasonable.

6. Make it work. The theatre manager is the only person in contact with all the elements of a production—onstage, backstage, and front of house. It is your job to bring all those elements together, and no matter what, remember, the show must go on.